RECLAIMING
FREEDOM

Coeditor-in-Chief & Publisher Deborah Chasman

Coeditor-in-Chief Joshua Cohen

Executive Editor Matt Lord

Assistant Editor Cameron Avery

Audience Engagement Editor Ben Schacht

Associate Publisher & Fellowship Coordinator Jasmine Parmley

Marketing and Development Coordinator Irina Costache

Arts in Society Editor Hannah Liberman

Contributing Editors Adom Getachew, Lily Hu, Walter Johnson, Robin D. G. Kelley, Paul Pierson, Becca Rothfeld, & Simon Torracinta

Contributing Arts Editors Ed Pavlić & Ivelisse Rodriguez

Black Voices in the Public Sphere Fellows Willow N. Curry & Kelton Ellis

Editorial Assistants Kian Braulik & Jack Ott

Finance Manager Anthony DeMusis III

Board of Advisors Derek Schrier (Chair), Margo Beth Fleming, Archon Fung, Deborah Fung, Richard M. Locke, Jeff Mayersohn, Scott Nielsen, Robert Pollin, Rob Reich, Hiram Samel, Kim Malone Scott, Brandon M. Terry, & Michael Voss

Interior Graphic Design Zak Jensen & Alex Camlin

Cover Design Alex Camlin

Printed and bound in the United States by Sheridan.

Distributed by Haymarket Books (www.haymarketbooks.org) to the trade in the U.S. through Consortium Book Sales and Distribution (www.cbsd.com) and internationally through Ingram Publisher Services International (www.ingramcontent.com).

Reclaiming Freedom is *Boston Review* issue 2023.4 (Forum 28 / 48.4 under former designation system).

Samuel Moyn's essay is adapted from *Liberalism Against Itself*, Copyright © 2023 by Samuel Moyn. Reproduced by permission of Yale University Press. All rights reserved.

Image on pages 1, 8, and 9: Roi Boshi/Wikimedia Commons
Image on page 90: Carol M. Highsmith/Library of Congress
Image on page 170: © Shane Young

This issue was supported by a grant from Omidyar Network.

To become a member, visit
bostonreview.net/memberships.

For questions about donations and major gifts,
contact Irina Costache, irina@bostonreview.net.

For questions about memberships, email
members@bostonreview.net.

Boston Review
PO Box 390568
Cambridge, MA 02139

ISSN: 0734-2306 / ISBN: 978-1-946511-79-9

CONTENTS

EDITORS' NOTE

FREEDOM IS a fundamental political value, central to any compelling vision of justice. And yet, as Aziz Rana notes in this issue, "a curious thing has happened within American culture. The language of freedom has been claimed almost entirely by the political right." Can it be reclaimed?

Leading our forum, Rana finds two conceptions of freedom competing for attention in U.S. history. The first—associated with extreme individualism—has staked the personal liberty of some on the unfreedom of others, both at home and abroad. The second—forged in movements against oppression—has imagined a more generous, inclusive freedom for all. The grip of the individualistic strain derives from some distinctive features of U.S. society, Rana contends. But its hold on American political culture is not absolute, and the way forward lies principally in building new institutions. To reclaim freedom, we need to "reshape the everyday worlds people inhabit," tying experiences of self-rule to democratic values of "mutual respect and common concern."

Some respondents extend Rana's analysis. Lea Ypi blames capitalism for creating new forms of unfreedom, and Philippe Van Parijs clarifies that freedom is a prerequisite for "fraternity," which he sees as the more fundamental political value. Other respondents consider particular institutions. Nancy Hirschmann and Tamara Metz focus on the family, while Adom Getachew looks to spaces for political education. And some disagree sharply with Rana. Mark Paul insists that institution building depends on political messaging, pointing to resources for a progressive narrative of freedom, while Jefferson Cowie doubts that the language of freedom can be redeemed—arguing instead for a focus on democracy.

Elsewhere in this issue, Travis Knoll recalls a movement that put the social emancipation of the world's poor at the center of Christian practice. Rachel Fraser and Will Holub-Moorman review recent books on free time and freedom from the family. Samuel Moyn revisits the work of Lionel Trilling to evaluate the legacy of Cold War liberals, arguing for a return to a bolder liberalism—one less haunted, as he sees it, by the conflict between freedom and totalitarianism.

Other contributors explore freedom in the context of particular struggles—from Black existentialism to violence in Israel/Palestine and state repression of social movements in Atlanta and El Salvador. Whether imagining social arrangements that might deliver lives of our own making or exposing obstacles that stand in the way, these pieces show how freedom remains an essential component of today's political struggles.

The forum in this issue grew out of two lively convenings in which many of this issue's contributors took part. We are grateful to everyone who participated, to Harvard's Ash Center for Democratic Governance and Innovation for hosting the sessions, and to the Omidyar Network for its generous support of this important discussion.

—Deborah Chasman, Joshua Cohen, and Matt Lord

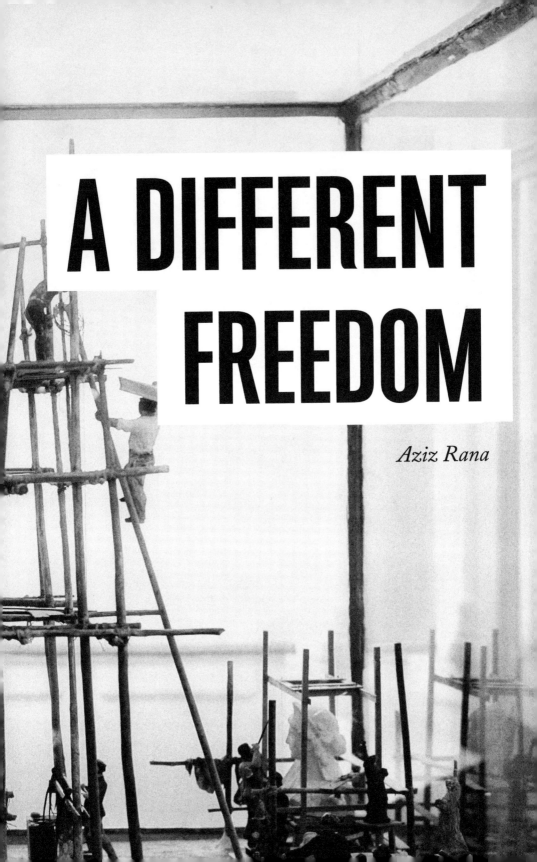

A DIFFERENT FREEDOM

Aziz Rana

THROUGHOUT THE WORLD the word "freedom" is strongly associated with the politics of the left. It brings to mind the great anticolonial struggles of the twentieth century, revolutionary battles against feudalism and aristocracy, movements for women's and LGBTQ+ liberation, as well as labor's fight to organize and to overcome workplace misery and economic oppression.

These associations are certainly present in the United States too. Many conceive of the civil rights movement as a pivotal part of a long Black freedom struggle, for example. But a curious thing has happened within American culture. The language of freedom has been claimed almost entirely by the political right, from the absurd (the renaming of French fries as "freedom fries" during the Iraq War) to the dangerous (reactionary House Republicans organize as the "Freedom Caucus"). Today, when many

Americans, across the political spectrum, think of freedom, they connect it to extreme individualism, market fundamentalism, bellicosity, and deep suspicion of social programs and government provision. Even worse, the right's capture of freedom has linked the word to resurgent white nationalism, in which proponents routinely present freedom as under attack from racial outsiders at the border or in the cities—and as requiring militarized violence to keep threats at bay.

One response to this development is to treat it as a matter of Democratic Party messaging. If liberal and left politicians better communicate their ideas, one might think, the language of freedom might be reclaimed. But the U.S. right's distinctive appropriation of freedom talk has deeper roots than political rhetoric. It is tied to persistent and structural features of *this* society—features made evident by placing the U.S. domestic context in a global perspective.

Specifically, the particular role that U.S. imperial power has played in collective life—both in the practices of settler conquest and in the terms of today's global primacy—has repeatedly emboldened exclusionary and highly individualistic versions of domestic freedom. This underappreciated context has shaped cultural environments in which it is almost second nature to link freedom to accounts of self-assertive and unencumbered individuals (coded as "white").

But the correct response is not to abandon narratives of liberty to the extremism of today's right, especially given the power of freedom as a political language both in the United States and abroad. Rather, we need a sustained political effort that would make left emancipatory accounts as culturally resonant and organically present within American communities as the ones they contest. And critically, such a project is not chiefly about communication strategy or political messaging. It is a matter of institution building, reshaping the everyday worlds people inhabit—their workplaces, neighborhoods, and schools—in ways that would naturally tie experiences of freedom to democratic values of inclusive solidarity, mutual respect, and common concern. U.S. history may have corroded notions of freedom, but that same history also indicates the conditions under which emancipatory language can be genuinely liberating.

ANGLO-EUROPEAN SETTLERS carried to North America a vision of liberty that in many ways remains resonant today. In particular, they argued that to be free entailed more than simply not having your immediate desires thwarted by others, or being subject to someone else's arbitrary whims. It required actually experiencing independence and control over the basic conditions of one's life.

In the economic domain, this meant both directing the terms of one's own work and enjoying security from worries regarding financial ruin or dependence. In the political domain, free citizenship carried with it the experience of participating meaningfully in the governance of society. Above all, to be free was to enjoy a robust experience of self-rule—an experience that combined a mastery over one's own life *and* a central role in shaping the direction of collective arrangements and institutions.

There are two ways this self-rule can be provided. First, a society can seek to elevate *democracy* to a universal and governing ideal across the institutional landscape of collective life. Members can appreciate the extent to which the profound connectedness of modern conditions means that no one can be free on their own. In the sphere of labor, independence requires the embrace of interdependence, in which all those that do the work—regardless of their wealth or status—enjoy shared control over the decisions that shape the workplace. Such an account does more than join freedom and inclusion together: it treats the struggle for a free society as only achievable through an ethical commitment to solidarity.

A second path, however, understands freedom as zero-sum and the world as marked by scarce resources. Under such conditions, my pursuit of material prosperity and my fulfilment of personal wants necessarily competes with that of others. For that reason, how I would like institutions to be run may well diverge from those around me. And if this is the case, then only those I view as similar to myself should have the power to make relevant decisions—or barring that, I should be exempt from collective strictures and common responsibilities.

Both paths have real roots in the United States. But the zero-sum account, more often than not, has won out, aided by the long-term nature of American expansionism. Even worse, empire framed these zero-sum competitions in explicitly racial terms. Land, for the early American settlers, was an essential precondition of economic independence and broader self-rule: in agricultural society, to own land was to be free. The great bounty of North America was a seemingly inexhaustible land base for economic prosperity. But in order for it to be used, it first had to be taken. Indigenous conquest and Native expropriation, then, became the basic engine of liberty.

Settlers' legal and political institutions were meant to do two things simultaneously. First, they were supposed to provide insiders with a robust experience of freedom. And second, to support this overarching project, these institutions were designed to extract much-needed land and labor from Native and then from other excluded groups, particularly enslaved Black people and their descendants. Thus, for most of American history, the dominant account of freedom was organized around two distinct and rigid views of governance— one for insiders and one for outsiders. Insiders enjoyed the benefits of political participation, the rule of law, and market prerogatives. Outsiders could face near limitless discretion and violence, whether from the state or from employers, landowners, and business.

THESE CONDITIONS linked freedom and domination together in racist and destructive ways. But critically, this settler story of freedom proved resonant because its beneficiaries enjoyed real material benefits.

Thomas Piketty notes in *Capital in the Twenty-First Century* (2014) that throughout the 1800s—indeed even during the Gilded Age—wealth inequality in the United States was "markedly lower than in Europe." He does not provide a proper explanation for why, but the answer is fairly evident. Across the century, the project of expansion provided white settlers with easy access to property. It cut against oligarchic tendencies within society, and facilitated a prosperous and small-scale brand of white capitalism. Settler society had its persistent class inequalities. But empire smoothed them over, making the experience of independence and self-mastery it promised genuine for countless white laborers.

The imperial backdrop fed a very specific and individualistic relationship to liberty. One did not necessarily need to embrace interdependence and collective solidarity to enjoy self-rule. If faced with land forfeiture or burdensome taxes, white Americans in theory (and often in practice) could simply move farther west and expand the edge of settlement. In effect, the idea that freedom could be entirely in one's own hands did not seem far-fetched. Government action to regulate settler society, then—whether enforcing debts or even seeking to contain, however marginally, white theft or violence toward Indigenous and Black people—was an unwanted intrusion.

Today we misunderstand this relationship to government as one that was antistatist or libertarian. Settler freedom far from opposed all government practices. Instead, the prevailing approach saw the apparatus of the state as a sword: one wielded by empowered Americans toward outsiders, meant to ensure insiders with unfettered control over private property and the enjoyment of self-rule. It was properly directed at Indigenous, Black, or Mexican people: never to be used against "true" citizens. Indeed, for white settlers, any internal exercise of state authority was nothing less than an attempt to reduce them to the condition of nonwhite outsiders—to treat *free* Americans as if they were colonial subjects. Generations of settlers thus came to see any constraint on their capacity to exercise power—including over the marginalized—as a dangerous threat to their liberty.

During the twentieth century the United States shifted roles dramatically, moving from a settler expansionist state with local ambitions to a hegemonic global superpower with far wider ones. American power was no longer organized around the idea that it had the right to claim new territory. Now, the narrative was that the United States rightly enjoyed military and economic primacy. Its interests were the world's interests, and therefore, the country had the right to intervene wherever anyone threatened to undermine the American-led liberal and capitalist global order. And, precisely because American power was exceptional, the United States—unlike other states—could legitimately move in and out of international legal constraints in the name of securing this order.

By the 1960s this vision of American dominance had rejected the explicit racism of the long settler experience. It now presumed that the United States was legally respectful of state sovereignty, regardless of the underlying racial makeup of the foreign nation. But in key ways, the terms of U.S. primacy still fed the same old domestic cultural resonance of freedom: one belligerent, zero-sum, and individualistic.

Abroad, the dynamics of U.S. power reinforced classic settler dismissals of what freedom actually meant for those on the global margins. With European powers decimated in the wake of World War II, the United States shifted from being one among a variety of global players to the dominant economic force in the world. Its currency emerged as the global reserve currency, and through the carrot of development assistance and the stick of military intervention and violent coups, it reconstructed foreign states in its image, opening markets for U.S. goods in the process.

All of this often went hand in hand with an account of racialized threat—just one that had been updated to fit within the new, more universalistic, narratives of nationhood and belonging at play. The new American global order continued to assume that the United States could exercise violence to fulfill its security objectives (read now as the world's objectives) to contain outside threats. And, as with the past, the threats primarily came from communities presented as less culturally and politically attuned to freedom—especially ones in the postcolonial Asian, African, and Latin American worlds.

In truth, the tension between the United States and decolonizing nations was often over substantive disagreements about what freedom *itself* entailed. Leaders like Michael Manley in Jamaica and Julius Nyerere in Tanzania conceived of liberation and self-rule as requiring a new system of "worldmaking after empire," as Adom Getachew has explored, in which all peoples had the genuine ability to shape economic and political terms. For instance, this meant bringing together a global majority around initiatives like the New International Economic Order (NIEO). Such efforts aimed to replace Cold War rivalry, and thus U.S. dominance, with a multipolar and solidaristic regionalism committed to overcoming exploitation and dependencies throughout the global economy. Yet time and again, U.S. officials read alternative frameworks—along with opposition on the ground to American interventions—through its own narrow security lens. Anticolonial understandings of freedom, when in conflict with U.S. objectives, were routinely dismissed as simply stalking-horses for Soviet power or evincing a racialized lack of "maturity."

At home, these developments promoted white middle-class prosperity, but in ways that reaffirmed the ties between external power and an atomized account of internal liberty. The rents the country was able to extract from the global arena—rents contested by Manley or Nyerere—meant that for many newly middle-class Americans, corporate well-being was equivalent to public well-being. This also meant that, unlike in other parts of the world, key elements of the American social safety net were ultimately left to what individuals could demand from the market. Jobs, pensions, and health insurance were all private entitlements for workers to negotiate from employers, not public goods entrenched through collective action and government provision. In this sense, as in the Jacksonian period of settler expansion, the nature of the mid-twentieth-century boom reinforced the idea that economic independence and material success rested primarily on individual hard work and entrepreneurial ingenuity.

In his wonderful history of labor in the 1970s, *Stayin' Alive* (2010), Jefferson Cowie quotes the son of a white steelworker, who recalled the dramatic material improvements and sense of independence and self-mastery his family enjoyed following World War II: "If what we lived through in the 1950s was not liberation . . . then liberation never happens in real human lives." This experience was real, meaningful, and in its own way worth celebrating. But at the same time, it was also the case that empire had effectively buttressed a cultural experience that one could be free *on one's own*.

TO THIS DAY American empire pushes domestic conversations about freedom down a corrosive path. But that path is not the only one. Indeed, the competing vision of freedom—the inclusive and solidaristic path—has at times gained the upper hand in American life, if only under very specific structural circumstances.

For starters, these ideas have tended to be strongest among those marginalized in settler society. A driving feature of the civil rights movement, for instance, was an exhortation to reconceive what freedom as self-rule meant. For those like Martin Luther King, Jr., the call for civil rights entailed more than simply ending legal discrimination and providing upwardly mobile Black Americans with an equal opportunity to achieve professional status and power. King saw American society as wracked by the "evils of racism, poverty and militarism," in which freedom for some entailed deep violence and injustice toward others. He argued that the country required a "revolution of values" and "a radical restructuring of the architecture of American society." This restructuring conceived of society as inherently interdependent: freedom rested on everyone's equal and effective ability to participate in the central decisions of collective life. Such a view demanded basic democratic changes to both political and economic systems.

King was not alone in these commitments. They circulated widely, from Fannie Lou Hamer's cofounding of the Mississippi Freedom Democratic Party and organizing of Freedom Summer to register Black voters across the South, to King, A. Philip Randolph, and Bayard Rustin's "A Freedom Budget for All Americans," and even to the more recent vision statements of the Movement for

Black Lives. It is no coincidence that Black reform movements have often—although not always, it should be noted—emphasized more inclusive and solidaristic accounts of freedom. More often than not, Black communities found themselves at the wrong end of the exclusionary version: the outsiders at the point of the sword. Racial structures in society subjected Black communities to state and private violence, and denied them access to individualized and market-driven benefits. The reality of being a minority in a majority-white society fostered the political need to link Black freedom to the freedom of all.

As for white American society? The most sustained period in which its inclusive and solidaristic accounts of freedom spread were in the early twentieth century in the years leading up to the New Deal—a period where the basic terms of settler life had collapsed. The frontier was closed; a hierarchical and extreme brand of American corporate consolidation had systematically replaced small-scale and more internally egalitarian brands of settler capitalism. More and more white Americans found their desires for independence and self-mastery thwarted by the unfree work of wage labor and tenancy. The political system further fueled this dependence, with a small coterie of corporate elites dominating public decision-making.

With this breakdown came an opening: new cultural and political space to infuse ideas of freedom with a universalistic, democratic ethos. The loss of their old privileges underscored to increasing numbers of working-class white Americans that freedom as self-rule required a sense of shared responsibility as well as common investment in democratic institutions like unions.

The collapse of settler expectations drove a growing willingness to push back against the worst excesses of its racism and exclusion, too. White laborers were more open to seeing themselves as having the same interests as Black, Mexican, and Asian workers: if their material interests were now bound together, then injustices to those communities imperiled white workers' freedoms as well.

These new realities further cut against that natural association of American power abroad with domestic well-being. In a world where the United States' global position had become uncertain—there were no new colonies to settle and the United States was not yet hegemonic—empire's relationship to domestic prosperity was less clear than ever. Some labor and socialist activists, like Eugene Debs or those in the Industrial Workers of the World, could convince supporters that whatever the benefits had been in the past, American imperialism now promoted plutocracy—not democracy—and enriched a wealthy few at the cost of freedom for most laborers.

These views eventually declined in resonance. After both World War II and the Cold War, American empire, and capital, were able to reconsolidate themselves, setting the terms for what counted as "freedom" in the process. This is not to say that they absolutely eliminated the cultural power of more inclusive and solidaristic ideals: indeed, the Black freedom struggle's great achievements came during the Cold War period. But the overarching structural context placed wind at the back of one path, just as it made promoting the other far more difficult.

WHERE DOES THIS leave us today? Freedom talk may, at present, be most associated with the politics of the right. But its account of freedom is actually less compelling to Americans generally than perhaps at any time since that early twentieth century. At present, there is a wide sense that most Americans experience nothing like freedom as self-rule. They are instead subject to the whims of massive and hierarchical institutions, at work and in politics.

The conservative response is deeply familiar. But the energy it used to carry with it is waning. More than ever, it feels like the right is falling back nostalgically on the same set of worn-out tropes that worked for them in the past. It continues to tie individualistic self-mastery to dismantling state programs and deregulating the economy. But even its own base now sees that corporate interests are not the same as the public interest. The mid-twentieth-century bargain with business, so good at the time at promoting an entrepreneurial, individualistic freedom, ultimately proved self-defeating, leading to much of today's precarity. As global economic conditions changed in the following decades, American corporations squeezed workers, abroad and then at home, and steadily eviscerated what remained of midcentury job, pension, and health care achievements.

In addition, nativist and white nationalist calls for more violence against perceived outsiders—whether detaining and deporting immigrants or backing police actions against Black and brown communities—appear to be little more than reveling in domination for its own sake. Such reveling has always been a psychic element of settler freedom, of course. But the present-tense embrace of domination is increasingly far afield from its historical twin: a guarantee that that domination would give genuine control to the majority of white Americans over the large structuring terms of their lives. As Robin D. G. Kelley has commented, Trumpism and the politics of the right today are notably "fragile." It rests on "ideological foundations" premised on the control of others but is now unable to make good on its slogans.

All of this is yet further underscored by the shift in the relationship between U.S. global power and domestic well-being. Today, fewer Americans than ever enjoy actual material benefits from the United States' dominant position in the world economy. And the projection of American military authority has, in recent years, gone hand in hand with disastrous wars in places like Afghanistan and Iraq. These wars were often framed by officials as centrally about the preservation of freedom at home and its spread abroad (hence "Operation Enduring Freedom"). But just as during the era of decolonization, interventions were routinely experienced by local communities as external impositions in deep violation of meaningful self-rule. And at home, trillions plowed into overseas conflict stood in sharp contrast to decades of disinvestment, a reality made even starker by unfolding health and economic crises.

Seen from the outside, the disconnect between what the United States considers its global security objectives and how many in Asia, Africa, and Latin America understand the ongoing legacy of colonialism remains a persistent tension. This dynamic is at play yet again in the Biden administration's actions following Hamas's October 7 atrocities against civilians in Israel. As many across the Global South see it, the United States is backstopping the Israeli government's devastating bombing campaign in Gaza, along with intense crackdowns in the West Bank and elsewhere—aiding another catastrophic war, while ignoring underlying Palestinian grievances and popular desires for equal dignity and self-rule.

As difficult as these times are, this unsettled reality does again open, however partially, space for more inclusive and solidaristic ideas of freedom. Younger Americans' growing embrace of the once-forbidden label of "socialism" and the broader political revival of social democratic politics underline the disenchantment both with American-style capitalism and with the political truisms about U.S. power promoted during and after the Cold War.

But this moment differs in crucial ways from those earlier periods of left-wing vibrancy. Activists today operate on a political terrain dramatically altered by neoliberal ascendance and decades of Reaganite cultural and political dominance. These changes have fundamentally eroded both the vitality and everyday presence of the institutions, chief among them unions, that once brought working people into the left. Why is this significant? Because if a left freedom project assumes that self-rule is a continuous exercise in participation and collective power, there are vanishingly few sites in American life—at work or in politics—where these experiences actually exist. We are simply not raised in cultural worlds in which collective agency is a meaningful reality.

The result, unsurprisingly, is that when invoked by left activists, solidaristic and democratic accounts of freedom can often seem theoretical and abstract; they do not connect to the daily features of one's life. Indeed, it is telling that today, the most potent left invocations of freedom overwhelmingly involve activists within marginalized communities who are referencing actual direct, immediate, and ongoing threats, whether in the context of racial justice protests against policing following George Floyd's murder, calls for abortion and reproductive rights in the wake of *Roe*'s overturning, or responses to reactionary attacks on LGBTQ+ identity and safety.

But despite these movement examples, the larger sense that collective self-rule and agency is not something regularly experienced can promote a pessimistic relationship to any language of freedom or emancipation. In fact, today's environment can leave some left-liberals wondering whether the longstanding and specific American relationship between settler freedom and racial domination is proof that *all* related narratives should be abandoned. Freedom in the United States as a discursive language, they warn, will inevitably collapse into exclusionary violence and subjugation. At the most extreme, this sensibility can generate a suspicion of the very utility of collective agency and even of political struggle.

But this sentiment must be resisted. It abandons to the right what has been a powerful and global language of social transformation: a language embraced, too, by many of those excluded from the dominant, reactionary narrative of freedom. And it fails to appreciate how in practice, ideas of freedom are always connected to those of subordination. Throughout the world, communities have come to understand the meaning of freedom in relation to the very modes of oppression—like slavery, colonialism, economic exploitation, or patriarchy—that are prevalent on the ground.

Even successful projects of emancipation do not overcome practices of domination once and for all. They generate new legal and political orders that knit together secured liberties with emerging hierarchies. Freedom struggles are thus forever ongoing. They may carry with them transformative, even revolutionary aspirations. But these aspirations are never completely redeemed in history. The American story of freedom and domination, then, is simply one way that knitting together can take concrete form. Rather than suggesting the need to reject such frames and narratives entirely, the complex U.S. experience highlights how we must grapple with our own particular histories and resulting combinations of freedom and subordination.

DOING so yields two main implications. First, it clarifies that the primary battle for the left is less about communications strategy and more about institution building. This means strengthening sites where individuals can enjoy collective agency and so would organically experience freedom as an inclusive and solidaristic practice.

Such efforts start with the political system, whose antidemocratic perversions feed pessimism in the very utility of collective solidarity and action. Expanding and equalizing voting rights—as well as reforming our distorted, state-based, and gerrymandered framework—all stitch together freedom and democracy in ways that cut against ingrained skepticisms.

So too do fundamental changes to the nature of the American workplace. Precisely because most people spend most of their time at work, the workplace is an essential pillar for reconstituting prevalent cultural narratives. Whether through bills like the Protecting the Right to Organize Act or other, more far-reaching endeavors, the legal terrain must be altered to expand the capacity of workers to join unions and strike. These workplace transformations should be properly understood as experiments in the linking of freedom and democracy: they make the institutions people inhabit on a daily basis far more amenable to collective self-rule and promote a continuous exercise in shared decision-making. The success of these efforts would create a fundamentally different ecosystem for political discourse and argument.

And second, the American experience shows us that any domestic vision of freedom rests on global conditions. What is often treated as foreign policy is not a sideshow: it necessarily influences cultural and political orientations in the United States. The nineteenth and twentieth centuries have taught us that we cannot expect an inclusive and solidaristic version of freedom at home if our government pursues projects of expropriation and expansion—whether over Native nations, still-colonized territories like Puerto Rico, or overseas societies.

This underscores the need to focus on reforms that integrate an anti-imperial ethic into how Americans understand their own everyday goals and interests. As with past efforts like the Freedom Budget, one key intersection is security spending. At a time when antiwar activism is cresting again at home and globally, the United States accounts for nearly half of all worldwide defense expenditures, with recent annual defense outlays of upwards of

$900 billion. This is a fundamental misallocation of the public treasure, one that bankrolls corporate militarism. It limits the funds available for the broad provision of economic security and independence—not to mention redistributive and reparative policies that commit to Indigenous freedom alongside genuine global well-being and equality.

Immigration is another central space. Whereas those like Trump link the foreign and domestic through racial demonization and a focus on the imperative of the border, the challenge for the left is precisely to invert and repudiate this framing. Immigrant workers provide essential labor sustaining American life, yet enjoy minimal legal and political protections. Transforming immigrant status would therefore go hand in hand with a profound reimagining of how economic and political self-rule can spread in American life. It would entail conceiving of economic independence and opportunity as divorced from the old settler duality between internal freedom and external power.

This approach rejects thinking of immigration as simply a matter that starts at the border, with virtually no attention paid to the particular histories, international economic pressures, and specific U.S. foreign and domestic policy practices that generate migration patterns in the first place. It carries with it an embrace of presumptive admission for all—the framework that throughout the nineteenth century defined the approach for European immigrants alone—and the basic decriminalization of entry. And the joining of labor and immigrant freedom opposes any closed vision of in-group solidarity, pushing both movement constituencies and Americans broadly toward richer accounts of shared class, social concern, and institutional arrangement.

Ultimately, there is no end-run around the hard political work of movement and coalition building. This moment instead requires a return to the essential project of revitalizing the institutions and social bases that would give meaning and power to any genuinely emancipatory narrative. Such a political project may not pay immediate dividends, but it is the foundation for real change. And perhaps most important, it offers a concrete mechanism for combining a language of liberation with practical improvements to people's daily lives.

TALK IS CHEAP
Olúfẹ́mi O. Táíwò

ON FEBRUARY 1, 1861, a Texas state convention voted 166 to 8 in favor of joining the newly established Confederacy and seceding from the United States. The declaration explaining this grave decision, published mere weeks before the first shots of the Civil War at Fort Sumter, listed a few grievances: familiar allegations that the U.S. federal government had failed to secure the states' borders with Mexico and Indigenous nations, alongside accusations that Northern states were subverting the letter and spirit of the Constitution.

But beyond these complaints, a central and organizing theme of the document was the state's abiding interest in the "beneficent and patriarchal system of African slavery," which the people of Texas had "intended should exist in all future time." For the secessionists, the "free government" established by the United States was not simply one in which racial inequality was permissible but one in which it was required. On their view, the claim that "*all white men are, and of right ought to be, entitled to equal civil and political rights*" involved a recognition that "the servitude of the African race . . . is abundantly authorized and justified."

What does freedom mean in a country with this political history? Aziz Rana highlights what he characterizes as a recent development in U.S. politics. As he sees it, the language of freedom has been largely cornered by its right wing, rendering U.S. politics somewhat exceptional to the global rule connecting freedom and liberation to left-wing politics. But as the Texas secession declaration exemplifies, and as Rana himself has explained in his influential scholarly work on the subject, U.S. history complicates this connection. While in other arenas the political right and center might coalesce around distinct values like security or economic growth, here freedom features as a watchword for abolitionist and Confederate alike.

There's much to agree with in Rana's essay. In general, the left's reticence to think and talk in terms of freedom and liberation reveals a narrow view of intellectual traditions and their possibilities—a point political theorist Lea Ypi has long made about socialist traditions specifically. But these very points are also reasons to be less concerned with the left's failure to embrace "freedom talk" as a "powerful and global language of social transformation." Rather than attempt a rhetorical or intellectual transformation, we should focus on other points Rana makes along the way: his calls for "institution building" and "reshaping the everyday worlds people inhabit" as ways forward for the U.S. left.

This focus would cast the historical story Rana presents in a different light. Whatever else settler colonialism was, it was a project rooted in dispossessing Indigenous nations of life and land and an economic strategy premised on making that land productive in important part by extracting labor from enslaved Black people. From that starting point—*after* the wars of dispossession, *after* the Middle Passage—it simply was, in fact, true that maintaining the political and economic rights of white "Insiders" required the domination of "Outsiders." The living conditions and political freedoms of white Texans were indeed premised on the subjection of Indigenous nations and the enslaved—but less in the way that a syllogism is premised on a starting assumption and more in the way that a house's stability is premised on the performance of a load-bearing wall. Abolition of slavery and the New Deal may well have prompted people to give a second look at a more solidaristic understanding of freedom as self-rule, but they did so in a specifically material and institutional way: by removing some of the severest obstacles to scores of people having meaningful influence over the course of their own lives.

This is why Rana's points about "institution building" ought to take center stage in both our analysis of how we got into our present unfree situation and how we can get out of it. As Rana notes, the experience of collective power and self-rule is one that is far from standard in American life. The decades of "neoliberal" and "Reaganite cultural and political dominance" that help explain why these spaces have eroded explain the lack of a solidaristic conception of freedom all on their own, and these problems are too deeply rooted in the country's developing political economy for the still-growing left to either think or talk our way out of.

Like any good leftist, Rana would agree that we have to organize rather than consciousness-raise or sloganeer our way out of these deep social and cultural problems. But it's worth reflecting past the mere fact that we should organize; we should also explain why doing so might work. Take unions. On top of the spreadsheet math that explains why either of us might get fired, and the interpersonal dynamics of shop-floor politics that explain why both of us hate our boss, landlord, or creditor, we can set the firm bond of a collective bargaining agreement. Joining a union—whether a workers', tenants', or debtors' union—does not simply make it more *compelling* that there are connections between your life's conditions and those of your union siblings. It literally *makes these things true* in a way that they were not before.

From this vantage, our focus might shift yet again. Rather than questioning the "freedom talk" that leftists do or don't engage in, we could ask first and foremost about expanding the ranks of the zones of collective power we seek to build—and, importantly, whether or not "self-rule" is really what people are getting when they arrive there. The recent culmination of the decades-long internal campaign for "one member, one vote" direct democracy in the United Auto Workers, alongside the broader victories this win has made possible, demonstrates both the importance and promise of cultivating meaningful self-rule in what spaces we can influence. Freedom has plenty of advocates; what it needs are construction workers.

CAPITALIST UNFREEDOM
Lea Ypi

WHAT DOES VIRTUE look like in the twenty-first century? Aziz Rana is right to point out that we need to focus on freedom. And as I see it, to reclaim freedom we need to revisit the relationship between liberalism and capitalism by reflecting on the pathologies that their connection has historically produced.

That's not easy. To the extent that liberalism travels with capitalism, it's a historical phenomenon, but to the extent that it departs from or qualifies capitalism, it's a social ideal. The social ideal is freedom, and the core promise is freedom from fear.

This idea is linked to a distinctive modern understanding of legitimacy, rooted in an analysis of the relationship between the individual and the collective. In the ancient world, legitimacy arose from the community as the source of moral norms. In the medieval to early modern period, legitimacy was linked to the role of the church and to the divine right of kings. In modern political thought, however, legitimacy is linked to a particular type of social relation: one grounded on the social contract. On this view, individuals who are born free and equal sacrifice their lawless freedom in the state of nature for the sake of the freedom that they acquire in association with others in a civil condition governed by laws.

There are many ways to understand this contractual relation, but the most promising focuses on relational freedom. On this conception, coercion by political institutions is only acceptable if we are equal authors of the norms with which we are asked to comply. This is the idea of democratic legitimation, and it explains why, in circumstances of emergency, only the state has the authority to temporarily suspend or to restrict the fundamental freedoms that it exists to protect: the freedom to move, to associate with others, or to vote in elections.

Most of these freedoms are guaranteed in the founding legal documents of existing liberal democracies. And most, if not all, of them were suspended or restricted as part of emergency measures during the COVID-19 pandemic. Many of them have also been at the heart of debates triggered by the successive crises: climatic, geopolitical, financial. What has become obvious is that the current economic and political system creates disproportionate burdens for particular social groups. Citizens of poor countries struggled more with access to COVID-19 vaccines compared to citizens of rich states; rates of domestic violence increased, too, and women paid the price. The cost of the green transition is much higher for the less wealthy. More people of color end up in prison compared to their white counterparts.

All this is to say that liberal society is not free from fear. In fact, in some ways it fares worse than the state of nature, in which powerlessness is evenly distributed. In liberal societies, by contrast, there are huge discrepancies in the protection that institutions offer to people who are equally subject to their authority.

Emergency rule sets a precedent for an unprecedented concentration of power in the hands of a few people. In the case of COVID-19, it was scientific experts. It could be data-controlling agencies. It could be economic and political elites who continue to rely on the authority of the state to demand obedience from all yet offer protection only to some. It could be social media in the hands of private corporations and beyond public scrutiny. For a few years now, the world has been in a permanent state of emergency: from financial crises to health emergencies, from terrorism to war. But as Machiavelli knew, Fortune shows her power when there is no virtue to resist her. Political emergencies, he insisted, are like the overflowing waters of a river. We need to take precautions "with dikes and dams when the weather is calm so that when they rise up again the waters ... will be neither so damaging nor so out of control."

My suggestion is that liberalism can only be rescued to the extent that it abandons capitalism. Otherwise, liberalism can't deliver freedom from fear, because liberal societies with capitalist economic structures produce pathologies of their own. These are different from the fear of despotism or intolerance that liberalism opposes, yet they are still destructive. They come in three basic types.

The first concerns moral anthropology. Liberalism released individuals from the constraints of traditional authority and celebrated the rise of civil society. The promise that each could pursue their individual good and that private vices would become public virtues was founded on the idea that trade could contribute to growth and material well-being. But as eighteenth-century critics of commercial society saw, there were also detrimental psychological traits that developed as liberalism intertwined with capitalism. Jean-Jacques Rousseau only listed some: self-centeredness, avarice, jealousy, mistrust, competition for nonessential and luxury items, a fixation on appearances, a yearning to make an impression, a dependence on external approval, rivalry, indifference to the plight of the most vulnerable. In the age of TikTok and Instagram, these phenomena can be observed in their naked form.

The second concerns economic theory. Many liberals recognized that rights were essential and that the state had the responsibility to guarantee the proper functioning of commercial society. But the state also relies on the allocation of resources by markets to fulfill its functions. In other words, the state depends on taxation and the financial contributions of the wealthy, and as rights become contested, class divisions reappear. To maintain domestic order, the state needs to rely on the international credit and debit system, which can mitigate domestic inequality by contributing to global anarchy. Indeed, as many early critics of liberalism, including Johann Gottlieb Fichte, pointed out, to secure its position on the international sphere, the state needed to expand its influence outward, encouraging war, colonial exploitation, and the depletion of global resources.

This leads to the third pathology, concerning politics. Classical liberals embraced a progressive view of history, believing that the global expansion of civil society would bring about prosperity and unlimited technological development. Enlightenment thinkers like

Adam Smith or Immanuel Kant saw history as a progression through different stages of production, from hunter-gatherer, pastoral, and agricultural societies to the more advanced commercial society. Yet this narrative inherently contained hierarchical elements. The price of liberal optimism in the success of civil society was the condemnation of alternative systems of production as inferior and the people adhering to these social structures as backward.

In this context, liberalism generated its own unique concern: the fear of colonialism and empire. This was not merely an unintended side effect or an inconsistent application of liberal principles, but rather a fundamental aspect of the liberal mission to bring the virtues of civil society to those considered incapable of realizing them otherwise. Liberals, particularly those committed to capitalism, often downplay the significance of colonialism, which they see as an unfortunate accident of history. In fact, as Rana notes regarding the U.S. experience of freedom, the two are deeply intertwined.

Without recognizing the link between the capitalist vision of commercial society and liberalism's civilizing mission, we struggle to understand why even progressive liberals like John Stuart Mill and Alexis de Tocqueville, who may not have condoned capitalism, found themselves determined to eliminate what they regarded as barbaric ways of life. Their motives were not accidental but integral to the liberal moral outlook and the aspiration to realize global commercial society, along with its associated structures and values.

The upshot of these pathologies is that, in its combination with capitalism, liberalism grapples with an inherent contradiction. On the one hand, liberals strive to curtail the power of the state, religious authorities, and other hierarchical institutions that threaten individual freedom. Yet in liberalism's efforts to distribute power, the project gives rise to distinctive power structures, fears, and forms of unfreedom.

These liberal power structures are depersonalized and spontaneous rather than planned. Psychologically, they breed selfishness and indifference rather than outright aggression. Yet these facts do not diminish the gravity or pervasiveness of the fears the project generates. If anything, capitalist unfreedom is even more insidious than the unfreedom it replaced. After all, where power is dispersed, spontaneous, and anonymized, it becomes far more difficult to confront. This is why people who care about freedom are looking for an alternative system that tries to decouple liberalism from capitalism—focusing not only on alternative economic and political institutions, but on the discourse of freedom itself.

DEMOCRACY OVER FREEDOM
Jefferson Cowie

RANA AND I agree on far more than we disagree about the history of freedom in the United States. My recent work on white freedom in one Alabama county confirms that American freedom often took the form of unconstrained capacity to wield power over the land, labor, and political rights of marginalized people. We both also see that attempts to curb that freedom to dominate were seen as an assault upon the deeply held ideological commitment to Jeffersonian and Jacksonian freedoms to dominate the land and labor of others.

But we disagree on the future. Rana urges that, despite the power of the nastier, master-race version of freedom—and the limited success of its more emancipatory meanings, at least within the United States—the idea is too important and too galvanizing a vision to be surrendered to those who wield it oppressively. In contrast, I find that freedom has been wielded too often in opposition to democracy to be of central value moving forward. In place of vague and contested "freedom talk," I advocate for building robust frameworks for democracy—a project that contrasts with, rather than complements, much of the practice of American freedom.

We can begin by recognizing that the roots of freedom were fraught from the get-go. Freedom is not just an exemplary political ideal twisted and corrupted by American slavery and land dispossession (although it is that); it dates back to problematic ancient republican values. To be free was to not be a slave, but a free person also held the power to enslave. Fast forward, and place that idea in a settler colonial and chattel slave society, and we find, as sociologist Orlando Patterson puts it, a people who are "free to brutalize, to plunder and lay waste and call it peace, to rape and humiliate, to invade, conquer, uproot, and degrade." To have a society based on freedom with scarce *fraternité* or *égalité* is to choose only the oppressive corner of the trinity of social struggle. Along with Fred Moten, I have to conclude, "Freedom is too close to slavery for us to be easy with that jailed imagining."

The story didn't get better. As Annelien de Dijn argues in *Freedom: An Unruly History* (2020), the participatory, liberatory version of freedom was aggressively attacked following the Atlantic revolutions. As democracy broke out, the antistatist version of freedom was weaponized to curtail the unruly democratic expressions of the people. As she puts it, freedom was mobilized not as a source of liberation but as a "formidable reaction against democracy." If we take this broad-brush idea seriously, then the history of freedom is less about the dialectics of different versions of freedom, as Rana argues, than a tension between freedom and democracy. To subsume democracy under the banner of freedom is to risk eclipsing democracy itself.

Cowie

In the United States, there is a long history of local elites using the idea of freedom to dominate others. They mobilized freedom, for instance, in their demand for secession after the election of Lincoln. "Will Alabamians permit abolitionists to rule them?" they asked. "Shall we yield like slaves or resist like freemen?" To not have slaves was to not be free. They denied the possibility of biracial citizenship by declaring for white freedom. It's also what they did a generation earlier during land dispossession, and later while fighting federal powers during Reconstruction, questioning key aspects of the New Deal, and putting up massive resistance to modern-day civil rights. White elites rarely invoked any kind of democracy since it was a threat to their power. Freedom was their path to it.

I am particularly alarmed by Rana's sense that by eschewing freedom we lose the entire vision for a better future. "Some left-liberals," he argues, may approach the "longstanding and specific American relationship between settler freedom and racial domination" as "proof that *all* related narratives should be abandoned." The mistake here is to think that democracy is inseparable from freedom, not a challenge to its profoundly knotty problems. "At the most extreme," Rana continues, challenging freedom "can generate a suspicion of the very utility of collective agency and even of political struggle." I completely disagree. By drowning democracy in freedom, he loses an idea that, almost alone, can fight the pernicious aspects of the American creed.

What are the ends of "freedom"? Here we run into further trouble. Rana's ends are a "matter of institution building, reshaping the everyday worlds people inhabit." Sound thinking, for sure. But the major democratic reforms in the United States—Reconstruction, the New Deal, the civil rights movements—built institutions that required enormous amounts of federal coercion (properly called "police powers"), which were and are seen as a form of antifreedom for the dominant culture. There is a reason that voting laws in the nineteenth century were often called "force bills"—because they were forcing the powerful to act democratically. A government that enforces laws and institutions will forever be the usurper of the freedoms of the powerfully entrenched. Yet as the historian Gregory P. Downs argues, "A government without force means a people without rights."

In essence, Rana's model pits different kinds of American freedom against one another: Black freedom secured by federal Reconstruction laws versus white freedom to dominate without fear of federal bayonets; New Deal positive freedoms versus Lochner-era negative freedoms; Martin Luther King, Jr.'s freedom versus George Wallace's freedom; labor's freedom to organize versus Reagan's freedom from the state. At best we are left with a vacuous category that might be filled with meaning and mobilized for good; at worst, it weds freedom to the deep history of the freedom to steal land, the freedom to enslave, and the freedom to control the political power of others. We might, as Rana would like, imagine a corrected, inherently didactic, version of freedom. That would mean a lot of effort explaining that "necessitous men are not free men" (as FDR put it), what the Four Freedoms mean, what positive liberty means—that our enemies' freedom means this while our version of freedom means that.

Yet why continue an exhausting fight to patrol the proper definitional lines of freedom?

Certainly the word has been key to emancipatory struggles worldwide, and there is a rich and inspiring history of imagining freedom without subordination, domination, or empire. But all that feels like a rearguard effort in what has become a kind of burned-over district in the fight over the meanings of the idea. The opportunity costs of preserving some "true" or "progressive" or "international" ideal of freedom are substantial, and they undermine a deeper struggle: the one over democracy.

Democracy requires embracing limits to one's freedoms in order to accept the citizenship claims of others. It requires an investment in the political infrastructure that curtails the freedoms of many. Democracy demands that we embrace the burdens of civic engagement, not the freedom to secede from them. It requires curbing individual liberties in order to respect the rights of others. It's about responsibilities, obligations, and commitments to a social fabric, not just rights and liberties. Democracy contrasts with the entrenched idea of white American freedom that sees federal power as an illegitimate actor, a violator of the freedoms of the dominant classes. Democratic culture, institutions, and practices require coercive federal powers, compromise, and regulation—the opposite of what many think of when they invoke freedom today. We need what might be thought of as a Hamiltonian democracy with a robust state system to ensure fair and equitable democratic procedures.

Paradoxically, Rana and I agree that the project is to reclaim democracy—to "elevate" it "to a universal and governing ideal across the institutional landscape of collective life." But why do so under the messy, often ugly, always contested, banner of freedom? If we have the institutions of democracy, freedom will take care of itself. On its own, "freedom" presents too much of an escape route: an invitation to run from the constraints of democracy, to flee the burdens of community and mutual respect, or to abdicate political responsibility by erecting authoritarianism, claiming, as Donald Trump did, that "freedom unifies the soul."

We could, theoretically, compromise and demand something we might call "democratic freedom"—offering a natural modifier that might help inoculate against the many types of antidemocratic freedom that have gripped much of the history of the United States in recent decades. But again, the project becomes a matter of policing language, not of creating a culture or building institutions. It is sobering to think that even under Rana's paradigm, the authoritarian Freedom Caucus is justified in using the term. Let them have it.

A POLITICAL EDUCATION

Adom Getachew

AZIZ RANA makes two interrelated points in service of generating a progressive and universal vision of American freedom. First, he illustrates that any effort to reimagine the domestic face of American freedom must contend with U.S. imperial power, which shapes and constrains the possibility for realizing any progressive project. Second, he argues that the left's task is not one of simply broadcasting an alternative to the right's exclusionary and domineering account of freedom but of building institutions in which citizens come to inhabit and experience their own political power.

I think he's right, and in fact, one way to link the internationalism of the first point to the institution building of the second is to consider the task of political education, which has always been central to progressive and left institutions. Despite significant ideological differences, early twentieth-century political organizations—from the Industrial Workers of the World, the Socialist Party, and the Communist Party to the Black nationalist Universal Negro Improvement

Association (UNIA)—were united in foregrounding this task. In the era of mass politics, the shared project of these otherwise competing political visions was how to transform the "mass"—a politically inchoate and socially variegated group—into a political agent, an empowered collectivity.

The education that this transformation required didn't follow the prevailing model of classroom instruction, with the solitary teacher at the front of the room, drilling her students. It was instead a collective practice aimed at both arming the masses with the capacities for recognizing their place in the world and producing a new sense of themselves as agents capable of worldly action. In publications like the *International Socialist Review* and the *Negro World*, the organ of the UNIA, readers were inducted into an internationalist analysis that located working-class exploitation and racial hierarchy in a global frame.

Weeklies and monthly magazines of this kind did not simply disseminate a party line to passive recipients; they were folded into collective readings and debates. For instance, UNIA members frequently read out sections of the *Negro World* during their weekly meetings, thereby reaching members who were not literate while at the same time transforming the solitary exercise of reading into an occasion for collective engagement. Such practices were supplemented by study groups, debating associations, and elocution contests in which UNIA members honed their analysis of the global color line and practiced their capacities for political speech and action. In the broad socialist, anarchist, and communist milieu of the time, workers cohered into a working class in everything from labor schools to theater troupes.

Political education was not only an ideological project; it also helped members develop a sense of political and collective agency. Instances of mass assembly from the strike to the parade were the high points of forging a sense of political power. In witnessing oneself as a member of an empowered collective taking up public space and contesting political power, one came to experience the meaning of individual and collective self-rule. Equally important, however, were the everyday ways that parties, unions, and organizations provided occasions to practice capacities of organizing and leadership. Legendary organizer Sylvia Woods began her political education in the UNIA chapter in New Orleans, where her trade unionist father was a member. When she was just ten years old, in 1919, Woods began to attend weekly UNIA meetings with her father, who encouraged her to listen closely to the woman who opened each meeting. She later recalled that her father wanted her to "hear every word" and would ask her to repeat the speech when they returned home. "We have to have speakers in order to get free," Woods's father believed. Woods would recite the speech at home, mirroring the woman's "voice, all of her movements, and everything." This formative experience informed her later organizing efforts with the Laundry Workers Union and a United Auto Workers local.

Rana is right that a key site for reactivating institution building on the left must be labor unions, which even in their decline continue to play a significant role in working-class political education. Political scientists Paul Frymer and Jacob Grumbach have shown that union membership stems racial resentment among white workers. In addition to improving the material conditions of working-class life, unions also change the ways their members see the world. As a member of the graduate union at Yale, I saw this feature of labor organizing in action. The labor federation in New Haven included white-collar workers and graduate students, who were primarily white, alongside a predominantly Black local of custodial and dining workers and a community organizing arm led by queer youth of color. These experiences engendered new solidarities across lines of age, race, class, gender, and sexuality. Anyone who has participated in a labor organizing culture can speak to some version of this experience.

While struggling to expand and bolster union organizing through efforts like the proposed Protecting the Right to Organize Act, progressives and union organizers should also be concerned with deepening the political culture of unions—transforming the union hall into a multifaceted site of political education that is embedded in its members' lives and a key part of the communities in which they live. We can learn from the UNIA Liberty Halls, party meetings, and union halls of the interwar period, where political education as an ideological and practical form of collective instruction was central to forging a sense of political power among working-class people. But the content and form of that political education must be reimagined for our own times.

The range of organizations involved in progressive political education during the interwar period also makes clear that the left needs to rethink other membership-based organizations. The Movement for Black Lives and the Bernie Sanders campaign have contributed to the proliferation of new organizations such as Rising Majority and energized older formations like Dream Defenders and the Democratic Socialists of America. We should continue to imagine how these organizations can embed themselves in everyday life and provide occasions for members to reimagine their world and their place within it. To realize the progressive vision of freedom as self-rule that Rana calls for—"a mastery over one's own life *and* a central role in shaping the direction of collective arrangements and institutions"—we have to build and multiply the institutional spaces in which working people instruct themselves in the analysis, habits, and practices of that self-rule.

FREEDOM MEMES
Elisabeth R. Anker

RON DESANTIS loves freedom. The governor of Florida—whose recent book is titled *The Courage to Be Free*—uses the word to describe many of his prized policies. The Individual Freedom Act, which helped cement him as a national figure, prohibits Florida public schools from teaching about racism. His second inaugural address, in which he declared "freedom lives here," highlighted his Parental Rights in Education bill, which prohibits discussion of gender or sexual orientation in public schools. And his 2023 "Framework for Freedom" budget was proposed alongside calls to ban abortions past six weeks, block transgender children from gender-affirming health care, and strengthen DeSantis's own freedom to speak without consequences by weakening laws protecting journalists. These bans, DeSantis argues, would make Florida "the freest state in America."

It might seem easy to dismiss the governor's claim that these laws grant anything like real freedom. After all, freedom is the most celebrated value in the American political lexicon; it entails independence, self-determination, and nondomination, and even across its different uses signifies the highest moral ideals and political aspirations. But Aziz Rana shows us that fully understanding freedom requires us to take people like DeSantis at his word. We need to realize that his policies *do* showcase freedom—one grounded in the ability to cause harm and exercise brutality. These capacities are intrinsic to certain forms of freedom in American politics, where freedom is enacted not only as individual autonomy or self-governance but also as the oppression of others. When he invokes "freedom" to support authoritarianism, racism, and sexual control, DeSantis is not using the term as mere ideological cover.

Nor is he being particularly original. Throughout U.S. history, practices of freedom have included enslavement and exploitation alongside independence and emancipation. The American Revolution, a galvanizing enactment of collective freedom for colonists who declared independence from monarchical rule, was also, Rana shows, a brutal and destructive process of Indigenous dispossession. In the antebellum United States, enslavers maintained the freedom of economic independence, personal sovereignty, and absolute domination through the lifelong exploitation of Black Americans. And well into the twentieth century, married men legally practiced domestic violence as part of their freedom; their liberty was the capacity to control, restrain, and beat their wives. In the 1960s, the infamous segregationist George Wallace described white supremacy as "the ideology of our free fathers." As historian Jefferson Cowie has shown, many Americans during this time resisted integration in the name of practicing their own freedom. DeSantis's Florida is a direct descendant of this history.

These practices exemplify what I have called "ugly freedoms": freedoms for some that depend on the oppression and domination of others. We fail to see the ugliness of freedom if we presume it is only ever a positive ideal.

We therefore need to de-idealize freedom, but not only from the right. Rana asks us to reclaim left lineages of collective freedom for a "profound reimagining of how economic and political self-rule can spread in American life." For him, this entails dramatic institutional transformation. But even this vision can overidealize freedom, associating it with courageous subjects, inspiring actions, or the decisive achievement of collective self-determination. This view occludes many of the mundane but still worthwhile freedoms present in everyday life: practices that are not grand and upright but nonetheless do generative work to fight for a world without exploitation or domination. If we want our descriptions of freedom to "connect to the daily features of one's life," as Rana urges, then we might start by looking here—at the freedoms far removed from self-mastery, brave resistance, or triumphant emancipation.

An example of a distinctly nonideal form of freedom can be found in online criticism of DeSantis. While on a trip to inspect damage caused by Hurricane Ian, the governor was photographed wearing goofy white boots. DeSantis might have meant for the photo op to portray him as a heroic protector of freedom, but memes soon made him into the butt of a joke, juxtaposing the photo with images of feminized figures in go-go boots. On the one hand, nothing might signify freedom less than a juvenile meme, which carries no real political power and takes little courage to post—especially a meme that associates feminization with shame. On the other hand, the circulation of these memes did something potent: through a viral display of mockery, it refused to let DeSantis claim the dignified ground of respectable authoritarian power. Shared by queer teens, angry Floridians, professional trolls, organized political opponents, dispirited teachers, and others, the memes built spontaneous networks of critique that undermined the ethos of masculine power and authority on which DeSantis's politics relies.

This banal and noncathartic exercise of freedom—the freedom to taunt an authoritarian leader—worked alongside more iconic forms of freedom in mobilization: organized movement protests in the streets, legal challenges filed by social justice lawyers, and sit-ins at the governor's office. The memes were not necessarily politically galvanizing, and they certainly did not overthrow DeSantis's agenda on their own. But in their own compromised, commonplace, and perhaps even cringe way, they gave many people—some who may have felt they otherwise lacked power or voice—a new way to work alongside others to oppose domination. More than something like the individual acts of resistance described in James C. Scott's *Weapons of the Weak* (1985), these actions crafted solidarity among disparate people who walked together on the low road to spoil the national narrative of DeSantis's unstoppable power.

Acknowledging this kind of freedom is not to narrow its horizon to small changes or to reject grander dreams, but to recognize that freedom inheres in more than exemplary or profound action. Finding freedom in the lowbrow, the low-key, and the low road expands our view to include actions and alliances dismissed as too ineffectual to build common worlds, or too petty compared to courageous acts of social transformation. It supports unglamorous, compromised, banal experiments that flourish within muted agency, uninspiring behavior, and radical dependence, to craft new possibilities for living free.

FREEING TIME

Julie Rose

AZIZ RANA highlights two sites where people's experiences of collective agency ought to be strengthened: the political system and the workplace. For those persuaded by Rana's compelling argument, I suggest a third realm in which freedom and democracy can be linked in people's everyday lives: their free time. Enhancing people's free time, supporting opportunities for people to spend their free time together, and infusing these social realms with inclusive and democratic values would provide people with ongoing and direct engagement with collective decision-making, from the very small scale to the more far reaching.

People are entitled to free time. To be able to meaningfully enjoy fundamental political, civil, and personal liberties depends on having access to the resources and conditions that enable their exercise—and these resources and conditions extend to time. In particular, people generally require time not dedicated to meeting one's own and one's dependents' basic needs, whether in necessary paid work, personal care, household labor, or caregiving. We must have time that is not consumed by the necessities of life, time that is instead free to devote to our chosen ends. And we must have it on terms that allow us to reliably make use of it.

Here I want to draw out three reasons why, in efforts that seek to strengthen people's everyday experiences of freedom through collective agency, free time ought to play a critical role.

First, and most simply, how much free time we have, the terms on which we have it, and the ways we can make use of it provides much of the structure and texture to our everyday lives. Rana is right to recognize the workplace as an essential site for revitalizing freedom "precisely because most people spend most of their time at work." But we shouldn't discount the time we spend outside of work and the time we spend navigating the demands from work and the rest of life. Experiencing collective freedom outside of work and in shaping work-life boundaries would go far toward connecting a democratic vision of freedom with "the daily features of one's life."

Second, to ensure that free time is widely secured requires looking beyond individualistic solutions and toward collective interventions. The causes of time poverty are multiple, and they can be glimpsed in a variety of situations: someone who earns minimum wage and who has a long commute because they can't afford to live near their work; someone who is squeezed by caring for their children as well as their parents because they lack access to high-quality, convenient, and affordable child care and elder care support; someone trying to keep up with a demanding career while also managing a time-consuming medical condition; someone who works long hours and would prefer to work fewer hours, even for a reduction in pay, but is unable to find work in their profession at shorter hours. All of these people might lack enough free time, and all would benefit from collective interventions that are attentive to people's time.

Providing free time on terms that enable people to use it effectively would also require a cluster of economic and social policy interventions. Most employees have limited discretion over their work schedules, and many have unpredictable schedules, as they must work variable hours, on-call shifts, or mandatory overtime without advance notice. Many, too, cannot count on their free time being protected from interruption, as they must constantly check for work communications and be available to respond. Those who must work antisocial hours—evenings, weekends, holidays—may not be able to coordinate their free time to share it with their families, friends, or communities. And just as we need free time that we share with other people, we also need spaces in which we can meaningfully spend our time, yet what we may think of as free time infrastructure—parks, recreation facilities, public and private gathering places—may be undersupplied or inaccessible. Addressing all of these elements depends on wide-ranging collective responses.

More broadly, everyone would gain in free time if we sought to limit the small intrusions on people's time that cumulatively add up—the "admin" or "sludge" of paperwork, navigating phone trees, and waiting in line—through reforms that may be as simple as automatic enrollment and prepopulated forms. As political theorist Robert E. Goodin and colleagues have argued, we might also benefit from downshifting expectations for personal care and home maintenance that ramp up our time demands by fostering a "culture of social equality." Further still, we might challenge the consumerism that leads people to work more to spend more.

Third, our free time provides vital opportunities to foster collective life and the practice of shared decision-making. When we spend meaningful time together—whether with friends and family or with those we share hobbies, recreational pursuits, or religious or partisan affiliations with—we inevitably experience, to some degree, what Rana terms the "need to embrace interdependence." If these social realms are infused with egalitarian values, they are likely to be sites where we have everyday experiences of collective decision-making. This kind of decision-making is unlikely to be the kind that devolves into endless, time-consuming meetings. It may take the more organic forms of a neighborhood's rotating potluck signup sheet or a knitting group's discussions about what they might contribute to a charitable cause. To create "cultural worlds in which collective agency is a meaningful reality," as Rana evocatively puts it, such informal collective decision-making is a vital complement to the essential democratic reforms in the political system and the workplace.

For all of these reasons, we should be attentive to free time—as well as political institutions and workplaces—if we hope to tie together freedom and democracy in people's everyday experiences.

AGAINST DOMINATION
William Clare Roberts

AS AZIZ RANA aptly notes, freedom talk can be hard to swallow at present—but not just in the United States. If a political party calls itself the "Freedom Party"—whether in Israel, Austria, the Netherlands, South Africa, or Ukraine—you can bet that it is on the far right. Rana is also correct, I think, that we should not "abandon" freedom to the right. But what exactly should a left "language of freedom" entail? Rana's answer—"self-rule"—exemplifies the most common response on the left: that the freedom claimed by the right, the individualistic freedom from interference by other people or the state, is not really freedom at all. *Real* freedom is democratic self-determination, or collective and solidaristic control of our common life.

I think this type of response is a mistake, for two basic reasons. The first is conceptual. If freedom is to mean anything, it must be separated from the use to which it is put. The way this point is typically made on the right is that freedom is not identical to virtue but is a prerequisite for it; the idea is that you cannot act virtuously if you do not freely choose to do so. In similar fashion, for collective and solidaristic self-rule—the left equivalent of virtue—to be possible and valuable, you must be free to fail to determine or rule yourself. To be free is to have a set of possibilities open to you, and to be able to choose from among them, even if that means choosing poorly.

The effort to construct a more "positive" theory of freedom collapses this distinction, identifying freedom with undertaking certain activities, like creative labor or active citizenship. In other words, theories that interpret freedom as self-determination, self-rule, or self-realization are not really theories of freedom at all, but rather theories of how freedom should be used.

The second reason is political. Self-rule can be given an expansive meaning, as in the emancipatory struggles of the oppressed fighting for self-determination. But as Rana traces, the concept of self-rule has often been weaponized against such movements by those with massive economic and political power. The dominating class portrays itself as a victim of tyrannical encroachment, while at the same time attributing to the dominated both the freedom to act as they wish and the responsibility to bear the punishment meted out by the shock troops of the status quo.

Thus Seneca, the imperial moralist par excellence, wrote of "a mere boy who, when he was taken prisoner, kept shouting in his native Doric, 'I shall not be a slave!'. . . . The first time he was ordered to perform a slave's task . . . he dashed his head against a wall and cracked his skull open. Freedom is as near as that." The point—echoed much later by Hegel, and then by the existentialists—is that except in very extreme cases, humans are inescapably autonomous beings. Even the enslaved rule themselves and are thus responsible for themselves and their actions. Even coercion does not override a person's freedom; it only gives a person a powerful reason to exercise their freedom in a certain direction.

This is a powerful argument against exercise being the right focus of a theory of political freedom. Exercising control over one's own life is a very low bar to clear: so long as you remain an agent at all, you are free on this account. Such conceptions of freedom leave us with no guidance as to which social institutions or interactions threaten freedom beyond the uncontroversial recognition that using physical force against someone negates their freedom.

For this reason, it is better to focus on what we want to be free from. I think the right answer is *domination*: the uncontrolled power of others to interfere in our lives.

Domination is not an abuse of power, but a power to abuse, and it comes in many forms. Your boss can throw you out of your job or your landlord out of your home, leaving you without a means of subsistence. Police can harass, arrest, assault, or even kill you. But crucially, the power to do these things does not need to be exercised in order to make us unfree. Women subject to male domination are unfree just because they have good reason to be afraid and must navigate their choices under the burden of this fear—a fear that arises not because women are not in control of their lives, but because they are not in control of what men can do to them.

What does it mean to be in control of what others can do to you? Certainly, you control what I can do to you when you can defend yourself against my unwanted incursions. Such direct self-defense is limited, but we can also identify a social form of self-defense: the countervailing power that gives others reasons not to harm us and protects or avenges us when they do. To be free requires faith that others aren't empowered to mess with us, and for this faith to be reasonable, we have to see others like us being supported and socially protected in this way. This kind of social security, which links freedom to solidarity, is the antidote to the anxiety and vulnerability of domination. That is why making robust social security—freedom from domination—universal is the historic mission of the left.

This mission is far from complete. Most people throughout human history have not enjoyed freedom, and most do not enjoy it today. Some have far too much power to abuse far too many. The right is correct that the state often has this power to abuse—even if they are usually wrong about who is most exposed to this power—but this hardly exhausts the range of domination. The state often exposes people to domination by *withdrawing* its protection, as when local law enforcement are allowed to inquire into immigration status, making reporting criminal victimization into a high-risk activity for anyone connected to undocumented immigrants. The poor, generally, are both overpoliced and underprotected, exposed to police harassment while also being unable to rely upon the cops to investigate or prevent crimes committed against them. Even if freedom is not self-rule, Rana is right that it requires that we build legal and political institutions that can extend social security to all.

How are we to pursue that goal? For the more reform-minded, extending freedom from the haves to the have-nots is a matter of institutional redesign and balancing existing powers. For the radical left, as Rana's history reveals, it is the liberation struggles of the dominated that open the path to universal freedom. Whether this project of building new institutions from below will succeed can only be settled in the pages of history that have not yet been written.

YES, FREEDOM!

Philippe Van Parijs

IN 1839 Louis Blanc, the French revolutionary from whom Marx borrowed the maxim "From each according to his abilities, to each according to his needs," wrote:

> Yes, freedom! That is what must be conquered; but true freedom, freedom for all.... It is because freedom has been defined by the word "right" that we have come to call free people who are slaves of hunger, slaves of the cold, slaves of ignorance.... freedom consists not only in the right granted, but in the power given, to a man to exercise and develop his faculties.

In the following decades, the theme of freedom—liberation, emancipation—remained present in the thinking, rhetoric, and action of the left, but it was often overshadowed by another theme: work, both as what entitles people to an income and what gives meaning to their lives. Being on the left tended to be synonymous with supporting the labor movement and its struggles for improving working conditions and increasing the labor share in the social product, whether directly, in the form of wages, or indirectly, in the form of social security entitlements earned through work.

Then came the powerful neoliberal wave, starting in 1949 with Friedrich Hayek's invitation to emulate the socialist "courage to be utopian" by offering a freedom-focused radical alternative, a "liberal Utopia." Milton Friedman popularized the idea that capitalism and freedom were inextricably linked. And then Robert Nozick and other libertarians claimed the quasi-anarcho-capitalist blueprint was solely consistent with respect for individual freedom: politically phantasmatic but intellectually fascinating.

Faced with this frontal attack, much of the left got trapped on the defensive. In the egalitarian project, freedom not only had to be subordinated to work, but also belittled, and even combatted, for the sake of equality. Aziz Rana argues that this was a mistake. Rather than "abandon narratives of liberty to the extremism of today's right," the left should revive a vision of liberty akin to Louis Blanc's, which he says Anglo-European settlers carried to North America: for them, Rana writes, freedom "required actually experiencing independence and control over the basic conditions of one's life."

I could not agree more. My *Real Freedom for All* (1995) was an attempt to debunk the libertarians' misuse of the concept of freedom, to help prevent the neoliberal right from appropriating it, and thereby to make room for the possibility of being both egalitarian and (truly) libertarian. Real freedom, understood more broadly than the republicans' freedom from domination, should not be viewed as a value in tension with the value of equality. It should rather be viewed as the *distribuendum* of the egalitarian conception of justice that the left should embrace. The left's many struggles should focus on reforming institutions in such a way that the real freedom enjoyed by those with the least real freedom should be as extensive as sustainably possible: in short, real freedom for all.

Such a left freedom project is often linked to demands for more effective democracy. Yet I would be reluctant to say, as Aziz Rana does, that "a left freedom project assumes that self-rule is a continuous exercise in participation and collective power." Freedom and democracy should not be conflated. Self-rule is not the same as collective rule, however democratic. In particular, while re-empowering the labor unions is a most sensible priority in the U.S. context, linking it *as a matter of definition* to the left freedom project runs the risk of reducing the appeal to freedom to a superficial facelift of the traditional "laborist" approach.

The contrast between the "laborist," or work-focused, left and the "real-libertarian," or freedom-focused, left should not be overstated. The former believes in the emancipatory virtue of paid work. Hence, for example, its plea for extending to women the traditional male ideal of lifelong, full-time employment. The latter, on the other hand, attaches as much importance to the real freedom to access meaningful jobs as to the real freedom to turn down or quit lousy ones.

Making freedom rather than work central has crucial advantages. It accommodates effortlessly the importance of nonlabor dimensions of life, such as the quality of public spaces, the health of the environment, or the fairness of intrahousehold arrangements. It does not fetishize paid work, which for many people can be an activity less fulfilling for themselves and less useful to society than what they would do if they enjoyed more real freedom to do something else.

And crucially, it does not induce a systematic identification of the objectives of the left with those of organized labor. In some countries, labor unions defend the interests of the best protected workers far more assiduously than those of the precariat. As unions tend to be more present in the public sector than in the private sector, they are often acting less in defense of the working class against the capitalist class than in defense of the interests of specific categories of public employees against the public interest.

Real freedom for all is not only important to the left's egalitarian project for the sake of justice. It is also important to economic sustainability. The real freedom afforded by basic income and other employment-independent unconditional entitlements is itself a productive force. The bargaining power such entitlements confer create a systematic bias in favor of training-rich jobs. The basic economic security they offer encourages risk taking and lifelong learning. And by widening the range of affordable options, they enable more people to find something to do that they like doing while being useful to society.

Moreover, real freedom is an important prerequisite for what might be regarded as the left's ultimate objective. For Louis Blanc, "true freedom" has not one, but two "immortal sisters": one is equality, the other fraternity—or, if you prefer, solidarity. Fraternity is about the quality of interaction between people: about what they voluntarily do for each other. So we can view justice as real freedom for all not only as an aim in itself, but also as a tool for bringing about fraternal relations. Such relations cannot be coerced into existence through compulsory labor. But a fair distribution of real freedom can prompt them. Countergifts can be expected in response to a fair distribution of unconditional gifts. If fraternity is to be fostered, freedom first needs to be regained.

FAMILY MATTERS
Nancy Hirschmann & Tamara Metz

TO RECLAIM FREEDOM, we need new ways to respond to attacks on democratic values and the resurgence of white nationalism. The family is key to this project, given the deep connection between the sort of freedom Aziz Rana criticizes and the ideological promotion of the isolated, self-sufficient, property-owning family that cares only for, and takes care of, its own: what we call "possessive familialism." Exposing this connection is essential to reimagining, revaluing, and reshaping institutions of care and family in the "everyday worlds people inhabit," as Rana puts it, and in the ways he calls for: toward "inclusive solidarity, mutual respect, and common concern."

Ideas about the family animate everything from immigration debates to health insurance to tax policy. The family is the rhetorical darling of politicians from Bernie Sanders to Donald Trump, and it is at the center of Joe Biden's response to the devastation caused by the pandemic: "The American Families Plan." Notably, this prioritizing of family might seem to conflict with what many would describe as the core ethos of the dominant neoliberal political landscape and its obsession with "free market" values.

What explains this surprising convergence of right and left rhetoric? We all need care. As political theorist Joan Tronto maintains in *Caring Democracy* (2013), care "is a species activity that includes everything that we do to maintain, continue, and repair our 'world' so that we can live in it as well as possible." In the world we have inherited, the family is assigned great swaths of this essential activity. But there are as many ways to organize care as there are families, and possessive familialism, which has deep roots in the liberal tradition, is only one of them.

It is well known that John Locke's politics of "free and equal" individuals rests on the "natural" institutions of money and private property—a vision that assumed, justified, and fueled the dispossession of the commons, land, and labor, the subordination of women, and the exploitation of the poor. Less familiar, perhaps, is the central role of the supposedly solo, self-sufficient family in Locke's account. Locke pays considerable attention to care in this family, such as paternal responsibilities to care for children, in his *Second Treatise* (1689). And in *Thoughts Concerning Education* (1693), Locke details a program for homeschooling, noting that parents have the greatest investment in the development of good character and "right reasoning" in their children because of affection as well as because sons will inherit the parents'—more specifically, father's—property. This "possessive family," like political theorist C. B. Macpherson's "possessive individual," is a necessary element of Locke's limited government and the liberal politics that supported the then-emerging capitalist economy.

The COVID-19 pandemic exposed both the influence and the impossibility of this model of care. Shelter-in-place and social distancing orders exposed the ruse of the self-sufficient family for many who had been able to buy their way into the fantasy. As social supports—from schools, soccer clubs, playdates, parks, housecleaning services, and restaurants to food pantries, basic employment amid layoffs, and access to extended care networks such as neighbors, grandparents, and friends—fell away, the early months of the pandemic exposed what many already knew: the possessive family is not capable of meeting the inescapable, unpredictable, and interlocking needs of care. No family, much less any individual, is self-sustaining: all depend on webs of interdependent support.

Though federal and state governments provided economic aid—a valuable resource for people who lost jobs, and one that enabled parents, generally mothers, to quit their jobs to devote more time to child care—they did not shift the structure of care in the possessive family. So the burdens of these responsibilities—online learning, extra housework, food preparation, responsibility for elderly parents, many of whom were also disabled—fell predominantly on women, especially those marginalized by histories of dispossession, enslavement, and exclusion.

As a result, women's freedom was sacrificed, not to mention their emotional and physical well-being: they fell behind professionally, and three times as many women as men dropped out of the labor force, the vast majority of whom were mothers. Far from an aberration, "the pandemic . . . revealed the extent to which mothers were barely hanging on in normal times," the *New York Times* noted. Of course, those mothers who could "hang on" at all were able to do so because of the vast networks of care—from undervalued garbage collectors to underfunded public parks and schools to underpaid nannies and home health aides—upon which they relied. Individuals and families, of all shapes and sizes, depend on webs of interdependent support. The fantasy of possessive familialism hides this fact, and by doing so, it naturalizes the structures of property, dispossession, and wealth transmission that fuel pervasive, ongoing inequality in the distribution of the benefits and burdens of care.

Once we expose and dislodge the myth of the solo, self-sufficient family, then practices of democratic care in which many are already engaged become legible as viable and valuable.

What would a politics that recognized these facts look like and call for? Start with feminist demands long ignored: high-quality, well-funded child care and year-round school, pay equity, paid care leave, more robust Earned Income Tax Credits and increased minimum wage, universal health care, and genuine "time sovereignty" policies such as flex time, increased vacation time, and reduced work weeks, as well as robust inheritance and corporate taxes, reparation initiatives, and well-funded housing support. Rather than weakening families, such policies will strengthen them by helping all caregivers negotiate competing demands in a global capitalist economy—thereby reducing stress and worry, making it less taxing to care for ourselves and other people, and simply giving people more control over their own lives. Public school curricula and public discourse that critically engage the histories of dispossession, enslavement, subordination, and exclusion that have made our present are also essential to a democratic caring and a caring democracy. Exposing the oppression that undergirds possessive familialism, this turn is key to seeing and supporting systems of care that make freedom possible.

Not every American will support such measures. Indeed, the radical right will decry them as attacks on the family—and freedom—rather than supports. What counts as family, who gets to form families, how those families are organized, and how government should support families—all these issues are major points of disagreement, and far-right claims of freedom such as those made by Moms for Liberty are curiously comfortable with oppression on this point. But these voices do not represent the majority of Americans. As the popularity of pandemic child support payments made clear, measures that provide real assistance to caregivers of every ilk are easier to garner support for than the reductions in defense spending Rana imagines. If such cuts were traded for spending that makes it easier for families to access the communities and resources they need, freedom would cease to be an obfuscating, defensive screed of the privileged, becoming a meaningful reality for all.

FREEDOM'S HIGH GROUND

Lorna N. Bracewell

THE FIRST TIME Florida tried to purge its swamps and seashores of what governor and 2024 presidential hopeful Ron DeSantis calls "wokeism" was in 1956. Reeling from the ruling in *Brown v. Board of Education* and eager to resist racial integration at any cost, Florida's state legislature formed the Florida Legislative Investigation Committee (FLIC) to surveil and harass civil rights activists. When the committee failed to link organizations like the NAACP to criminal activities or communist conspiracies, it shifted its focus to "practicing homosexuals" who they believed had infiltrated the state's public school system to seduce and abuse children. By the time the FLIC disbanded in 1965—forced to shutter, ironically, due to public outcry over its publication of a report widely seen as pornographic—it had orchestrated the firing, expulsion, or resignation of some four hundred public school students and teachers.

Twelve years later, recording artist and Florida Citrus Commission spokesperson Anita Bryant stepped in to fill the FLIC's shoes, founding Save Our Children, Inc.—whose mission was to repeal a

Dade County human rights ordinance that prohibited discrimination in employment, housing, and public accommodation on the basis of "affectional or sexual preference." Bryant's campaign picked up where the FLIC left off, painting gays and lesbians—especially gay and lesbian teachers—as threats to public health and safety. In the run-up to the repeal referendum, Save Our Children released an ad in the *Miami Herald* titled "The civil rights of parents: to save their children from homosexual influence," which claimed that discrimination against gays and lesbians is "no more a civil rights issue than is the arrest of a drunk for disturbing the peace." Appeals like this proved effective. On June 7, 1977, voters repealed the county ordinance by a more than two-to-one margin.

Since Florida's Parental Rights in Education Act and Individual Freedom Act were signed into law in the spring of 2022, pundits have drawn attention to the continuities between DeSantis's war on wokeism and the racial and sexual purity campaigns of earlier eras. But where the dominant motifs of the old wars were law and order, public health and safety, and state surveillance, DeSantis talks mostly of freedom, vowing not to protect but to liberate Floridians from the tyranny of gender ideology and CRT. This rhetorical shift underscores an important political lesson political theorist Corey Robin gleaned from his dissection of "the reactionary mind": conservatives learn from the revolutions they oppose. Indeed, they are often, Robin writes, "the left's best students."

During the great civil rights struggles of the 1950s, '60s, and '70s, there was much for conservatives to study up on. Black people, women, and queers were appropriating the language of freedom, then used mostly by Cold War–era anticommunists to defend the liberal capitalist status quo, to assail the hierarchies conservatives defended at the time through appeals to safety and security.

Harvey Milk's famous "That's What America Is" speech—delivered on June 25, 1978, the ninth anniversary of the Stonewall Rebellion, at San Francisco's annual Gay Freedom Day celebration—is one of many examples from this period of a champion of the marginalized wielding the language of freedom against a conservative language of protection and security. Milk opens his speech by asking his "gay sisters and brothers to make the commitment to fight. For themselves. For their freedom." Midway through the speech, Milk threatens President Jimmy Carter, whose support for gay rights he found tepid and insincere, with a March on Washington to be held, of course, on "that national day of freedom, the fourth of July." To conclude, Milk quotes the poem at the base of the Statue of Liberty ("Give me your tired, your poor, your huddled masses, yearning to breathe free") and the National Anthem ("Oh, say does that star-spangled banner yet wave o'er the land of the free") to remind "all the bigots out there" that "that's what America is."

Although Milk was assassinated shortly after giving this speech, the metonymy he helped create between "gay," "freedom," and "America" lived on, providing the framework for a movement that would win many victories: the nationwide decriminalization of same-sex intimacy in 2003, national legal recognition for same-sex marriages in 2015, and the enactment of hundreds of state and local human rights ordinances that now cover nearly half the U.S. population.

Given this string of queer triumphs, it is no surprise that conservatives like DeSantis are attempting a wardrobe refresh, waging the same old culture war in freedom-brocaded fatigues. They recognize that the only way to shove the lower orders back in their place is to first displace them from the high ground of freedom. Such efforts are more than rhetorical. DeSantis's policies connect his chauvinistic, atomistic, and zero-sum narrative of freedom to the kind of concrete experiences of settler self-rule that Aziz Rana identifies as so central to the right's ascendancy across U.S. history.

Take Florida's SB 252, a sweeping "medical freedom" law that prevents both private and governmental entities from requiring individuals to utilize even minimally invasive measures like face masks to prevent the spread of deadly disease. Under the law, every trip to the doctor's office or the grocery store becomes an opportunity for certain citizens—who view even the smallest act of solidarity as a violation of their natural rights—to experience the thrill of freedom as domination. Florida's Parental Rights in Education Act delivers an even more sadistic and direct experience of freedom as domination, empowering reactionary parents to dictate what gender identities, sexual orientations, historical narratives, and even books will be permitted in public schools, and turning every school board meeting into an opportunity to denigrate the sexualized and racialized others threatening their rights and liberties.

To the extent that Rana addresses the freedom politics of figures like DeSantis, he is dismissive. They are simply "reveling in domination for its own sake," he writes, and failing to give "genuine control to the majority of white Americans over the large structuring terms of their lives." He further claims that highly individualistic and exclusionary accounts of freedom are less appealing to Americans now than they have been in nearly a century because their material and cultural underpinnings have been eroded. "There is a wide sense," he writes, "that most Americans experience nothing like freedom as self-rule." That may be true in some places, but plenty of Americans in places like Florida are enjoying the fruits of a form of belligerent and bigoted self-rule, backed up materially through policies like Florida's HB 1, a voucher program that provides parents who remove their children from public school a payment of approximately $8,000 per child per year that can be spent on virtually anything. DeSantis and other so-called "national conservatives" have accurately diagnosed the limits of the neoliberal approaches to freedom that were once in vogue on the right. They are now undertaking in earnest the work of "institution building, reshaping the everyday worlds people inhabit—their workplaces, neighborhoods, and schools" to weave their conception of freedom into the fabric of people's lives in precisely the ways Rana argues are essential.

Rana is right to exhort the left to move beyond "messaging" and "communications strategy" and toward nurturing spaces where people can "organically experience freedom." But he misses just how far ahead the right is in this effort already. In order to catch up, we cannot content ourselves with dismissing the right's freedom politics as a disingenuous and purely rhetorical sideshow. To build sites of freedom that are inclusive and democratic, we need to confront the patriarchal, white supremacist, and heteronormative investments that make exclusionary and individualistic forms of freedom so appealing. Conservatives learn from the revolutions they oppose; it is high time the left started to do the same.

THE STORY OF FREEDOM
Mark Paul

AZIZ RANA rightly contends that the fight for freedom is more than
a simple narrative sparring match. Words are powerful, but delivering meaningful and lasting freedom requires building the institutions necessary to deliver the goods—among them labor unions,
high-quality public schools, and the protection and expansion of
truly democratic processes.

I agree that communication strategies alone are insufficient,
but in my reading, Rana goes too far by brushing aside the crucial
narrative work that must be done—work that is actually comple-
mentary to building the institutions, power, and meaningful freedom
I know we both seek.

The very idea of freedom is contested terrain—it is, after all, the
central political ideal of America, what historian Eric Foner calls our
"master narrative"—and this battle is not a new one. What we mean by
freedom has been fought over since the very founding of the United
States, and the nation literally tore itself apart over this struggle. Did

American freedom encompass the right to hold human beings in chattel slavery, thus denying any semblance of freedom to Black Americans? Or did American freedom entail the elimination of human bondage, along with the necessary civil, political, and economic rights to provide people meaningful opportunity to participate in democratic government and individual security? The Civil War, and later the civil rights movement, were momentous interventions in this struggle.

For the last half century this fight was pushed to the margins, sidelined by a new, largely bipartisan consensus over freedom. Capitalism seemed to many as though it would solve the centuries-long struggle; freedom now simply meant "free" markets, which in turn meant limited government—whether limited taxation, limited regulation, or limited oversight over local school boards. All this entailed some degree of political rights if you acted "right" and were part of the dominant group.

Today, with the utter failure of laissez-faire capitalism yet again— and the persistence of structural racism, despite false promises of achieving a postracial society—we have seen the rise of a more powerful and organized political left in the United States. At the same time, the far right has grown increasingly emboldened. In this conflict, the long struggle for freedom, and who has the right to be free, have center stage once more.

As this renewed conflict suggests, narratives are immensely powerful. It's true that we can't run some regressions to decompose the marginal impact of investing in narratives and how that translates to political power—at least not well. Nevertheless, investing our scarcest resource of all—our time—in narratives, ensuring voters know what a political party stands for, is invaluable.

When it comes to popular opinion, Republicans have clearly won the messaging battle: they are thought of as the party of freedom—the party that supports individual liberties and restraints on government. In reality, of course, much of the GOP does nothing of the sort, wielding big government when it suits them—from the law-and-order Republicans who funnel ungodly sums of money to law enforcement and the military, to the "family values" conservatives who expand government overreach by imposing abortion bans to wrestle away reproductive freedom from individuals. Still, the electoral power of the GOP derives in no small part from its rhetorical success: it has a simple message, and it sticks to it.

Now consider the Democratic Party. What, exactly, do Democrats stand for? In the popular imagination, their vision has become, at best, something like "not Trump," or "not neoliberalism." When President Biden announced earlier this year that he would seek re-election in 2024, he repeatedly invoked freedom, but it wasn't exactly clear what he meant and how this rhetoric connected to his policy priorities. This is a familiar line of critique; commentators routinely point out that Democrats are always touting a "laundry list" of demands without a coherent story that ties them together.

This is where I believe the narrative struggle is well worth the energy. The lack of a coherent and easily communicated vision among Democrats, and the left more broadly, poses a serious problem for building movements and institutions. What, after all, are people fighting for? And what type of institutions will help deliver on those demands? These are crucial questions that can be addressed by properly articulating a north star: freedom.

There are plenty of popular narrative resources throughout U.S. history that we might draw on to make this case. Thomas Paine was unshakable in his pursuit of true democracy—coupled with equality of opportunity and result in the economic realm—as the foundation of a new, and truly free, nation. Abraham Lincoln and the Radical Republicans helped achieve the abolition of slavery. Franklin Roosevelt championed what he called the "Four Freedoms" and called for an Economic Bill of Rights. And the civil rights movement likewise demanded far more than political rights by centering economic demands, for instance in A. Philip Randolph and Bayard Rustin's "Freedom Budget" and Martin Luther King, Jr.'s organization of the 1968 Poor People's Campaign.

These struggles provide the U.S. left with a narrative and a powerful historical connection to the American story that squarely posits the fight for a richer, more fulfilling notion of freedom as central to the struggle for the country itself. Meaningful freedom will only be won through embracing an emancipatory vision of freedom that guarantees people political rights, civil rights, reproductive rights, and crucially, economic rights. Together these rights provide people with meaningful choices to be, and do, what they have reason to value.

It is true that narrative change is not a silver bullet; it alone cannot bridge the gulfs that have widened as the nation has become increasingly polarized. But stories, coupled with the critical work of reweaving the social fabric of our nation and delivering meaningful improvements in people's daily lives through policy change, just might be. The terrain over the meaning of freedom remains contested, but the struggle—including the narrative struggle—is essential.

A GENUINE POLITICS OF FREEDOM

Aziz Rana

TWO DISTINCT THEMES emerged in these incisive and moving responses. First, how should we think about the relationship between political narratives and institution building? And second, what should we make of freedom's persistent exclusivities in the United States?

On the first point, let me clarify why I believe our focus should lie more on institutions than on messaging. Like Mark Paul, I absolutely agree that narrative and narrative change is vital to freedom struggles. But for narratives to be meaningful, they have to be organically connected to how people experience their daily lives. Lawrence Goodwyn, historian of the Populist movement, argued that the goal of left mobilization has long been to move people out of the "received culture" that shapes their lives to a "movement culture" that provides energy for transformative projects. These efforts require more than making arguments in the abstract about ideas of community or economic interest. They require a cultural infrastructure in which values—including those around the politics of freedom—are present in the everyday institutions that organize people's experiences.

For this reason, I strongly concur with Olúfẹ́mi Táíwò's conclusion that left freedom projects today most of all need "construction workers." It's also why I agree with William Clare Roberts's contention that the focus should be less on defending an abstract notion of freedom—say, as self-rule or otherwise—and far more on organizing those at the margins to contest their routine experiences of domination.

The great freedom struggles of the past have always been rooted above all in building the capacity of oppressed groups to call out the domination they face *as domination* and then to imagine and pursue horizons of change. In this way, notions of emancipation emerged out of concrete oppression but increasingly became galvanizing horizons of possibility—pushing mobilized groups toward ever more transformative ends. For communities on the ground, the meanings of freedom—even truly aspirational accounts of liberation—have only ever been understood in relation to prevalent forms of unfreedom, from slavery and colonialism to economic exploitation and patriarchy.

Several responses help to clarify how institutions matter—and what kinds of institutions we need to shift people from a received culture to a movement culture. Adom Getachew's compelling discussion of political education invites us to see workplaces, schools, neighborhoods, and other arenas of social life in a different light. Rather than thinking of these institutions as primarily about the enjoyment of individual or private benefits, we should approach them as places where we learn—through formal and informal educational initiatives as well as general community building—the meaning and practice of solidarity and politics.

At the same time, we must guard against a too workplace-centric approach. We see this in Nancy Hirschmann and Tamara Metz's powerful contention that the family has a central role to play in efforts at institutional reconstruction and thus in a more genuine politics of freedom. Given that the family remains the defining site for the cultural reproduction of a zero-sum and possessive individualism, reforms that shift the terms of the relationship between family, freedom, and care are key. In addition, Julie Rose's focus on free time highlights the role of time theft in imposing oppressive everyday experiences on most people. Reclaiming time is thus a meaningful way of shifting power relations in society as well as engaging in left organizing against actual daily forms of domination.

A focus on institution building further allows left freedom talk to avoid devolving into a language of romantic rupture or ungrounded utopia, as Elizabeth Anker worries. It focuses action on step-by-step shifts, even if small-scale, that make it harder for the status quo to reproduce itself. None of this is to deny Lorna Bracewell's powerful caution that reactionaries have made profound inroads wielding exclusionary invocations of freedom. Partly as a result, the relevant struggle is principally over who controls the institutional terrain— and is thereby able to shape which narratives of freedom are most culturally organic.

For all these reasons, I do not believe in a messaging silver bullet. But I am also opposed to giving up entirely on the language of liberation, even though I share many of the concerns about the history of American freedom voiced by Jefferson Cowie. For one thing, I am skeptical that the language of democracy would necessarily avoid the historical and political difficulties of the language of freedom. It is telling that Jacksonians in the nineteenth century called their party "the Democracy." The history of exclusionary settler freedom is very much also a history of white or ethnonationalist democracy.

It is true that today's reactionaries increasingly embrace minority rule; they question especially the value of *multiracial* democracy. This certainly opens space for claiming an inclusive democratic language. Still, it is worth noting that in the present the old Jacksonian ideas of exclusionary democracy remain culturally powerful—especially in debates about immigration and American foreign policy. We see this in justifications of the United States' draconian and militarized approach to the border. The systematic deprivation of immigrant rights is defended as a preservation of an internal, self-governing community—often coded as white—from external nonwhite threat. Similarly, defenses of the United States' right to project power and impose violence abroad—unchecked by multilateral institutions or international legal constraints—are bound up with internal democratic notions of sovereignty.

None of this means that democracy should be rejected as a powerful narrative—quite the opposite. Emancipatory versions of both freedom and democracy have had profound meaning, on the ground, for oppressed communities. They have given purpose and hope to those facing the extremes of exploitation and injustice. And taking seriously the values and vision of movement constituents and activists means similarly taking seriously the words—and the related ideas—that they have used in their collective struggles.

But transformation depends on background structural realities. Our goal must therefore be to develop interventions and organizing practices aimed at steadily dislodging the institutional landscape that sustains both hierarchy and domination. This is why I also concur with Lea Ypi's arguments about the corrosive effects of capitalism on narratives of freedom. These effects include precisely what Hirschmann and Metz emphasize: the formation of possessive and atomized political subjects for whom accounts of self-mastery are especially culturally resonant. It is also why, though I embrace Philippe Van Parijs's admonition to avoid reducing freedom to a brand of laborite politics, I am hesitant to separate freedom from a vision of democracy. By often deemphasizing an *equal and effective* freedom for all, such separations tend to fall back on the accounts Ypi so rightly contests.

In the end, I see the very real constraints on emancipatory uses of freedom in the United States as a product of history. They crucially depend on the position of the United States in the global dynamics of race, economy, and power. Any genuine commitment to equal and effective freedom for all runs up against the hegemony of U.S. power on the world stage, which in turn fuels deep currents of national self-understanding and collective pride. Arguing for universal freedom from the very heart of modern empire necessarily means arguing for a redistribution of power and resources away from that center and from those who have typically enjoyed these benefits. This is why so many of the left's great freedom struggles, at home and abroad, have come from people on the internal and external periphery.

But if history made this state of affairs, our shared struggles can also unmake it. However deep-rooted the structural predicaments, the effort to shift the infrastructure of American life, along with our collective self-understanding, remains essential. This certainly requires being clear-eyed about obstacles to change, and the forces that tie the discourse of freedom to practices of domination. But it also entails a sustained commitment to a politics of collective agency and solidarity that, despite the obstacles, can refashion the world on fundamentally better terms. This has always been the left emancipatory aim—one both internationalist and utopian in the best sense—and it should continue to be ours as well. ◆

SALVATION NOW

Travis Knoll

IN 1984, in the heat of the Cold War, leading neoconservative theologian and American Enterprise Institute fellow Michael Novak took
to the pages of the *New York Times Sunday Magazine* to denounce
the decades-old liberation theology movement. For its advocates,
the movement was a method that put social emancipation, not the
afterlife, at the center of Christian practice. For Novak, it was an
unholy alliance between Marxist ideology and Christianity.

Novak detailed how idealistic Latin American clergy, nuns,
and missionaries had all been duped by its fusion of religion and
revolutionary thought. It had swindled U.S. politicians, too. When
the likes of Speaker of the House Tip O'Neill challenged Ronald
Reagan's effort to cast the revolutions rocking Central America as
existential threats to U.S. security interests, they were relying on
liberation theology's distorted account of reality, Novak contended.
The stakes could not be higher. "If Marxism, even of a mild sort,
flourishes" in Latin America and the Philippines, he warned, "and

if it were to be officially blessed by Catholicism, two powerful symbolic forces would then have joined hands."

Novak must have heard how Fidel Castro had discredited a center-right Cuban Catholic hierarchy as "Pharisees" and "white sepulchers" during a fiery August 1960 address. ("To betray the poor is to betray Christ," Castro declared. "To serve wealth is to betray Christ. To serve imperialism is to betray Christ.") And he had surely seen the global outpouring of sympathy after the 1980 murder of El Salvador's archbishop Óscar Romero at the hand of militias once supported by a U.S.-backed government. Romero had been a relatively conciliatory bishop before assuming the Church's top post in El Salvador, where he grew increasingly frustrated with state violence and the government's broken promises of reform and embraced liberation theology's practical vision. Romero's political turn must have shown Novak what was dangerous about the movement: that it could radicalize the faithful, from young priests on the ground to members of U.S. Congress.

For Novak, one book in particular—"electrifying and seminal," he had to admit—encapsulated the movement: Peruvian theologian Gustavo Gutiérrez's *A Theology of Liberation*, published in 1971 and first translated into English in 1973. (The translation was recently rereleased in a fiftieth-anniversary edition by Orbis Books.) Born in 1928 of mixed Spanish and Indigenous ancestry, Gutiérrez studied in Louvain, Belgium, at the height of Francophone progressive theological influence in the post–World War II period; he counted among his classmates the Colombian priest and revolutionary Camilo Torres. When Gutiérrez returned to Peru, he sensed the excruciating disconnect between high theology and everyday realities. Surrounded by crushing poverty and anticolonial resistance, he grappled with where a traditional institution like the Catholic Church should stand in such a context. Out of these conditions, *A Theology of Liberation* was born, melding rigorous biblical interpretation, social science, and a vision for social justice.

In the United States today, organized Christianity is mostly associated with restrictions on reproductive autonomy, counter-majoritarian and white nationalist agendas, and an embrace of free enterprise economics—even though it has also played a central role in civil rights and progressive movements throughout U.S. history. *A Theology of Liberation*, by contrast, represents a tradition that put religious reflection at the heart of the struggle of the global poor. By embodying ambition instead of compromise, it also offered an alternative to the schismatic tendencies of multicultural liberalism.

The book is a product of the concerns of its time; it was published years before women and minority voices began to shape the terms of broad political debate. Some of the social and economic crises it combatted—military rule and armed revolutions—are thankfully, for now, in Latin America's past. But others—issues of economic dependence, political and cultural oppression, and glaring inequali-ties—remain, and so too does its influence.

A THEOLOGY OF LIBERATION combines multiple publications and talks Gutiérrez gave in the 1960s after the Second Vatican Council (1962–1965) and in the run-up and aftermath of its Latin American successor, the Second Latin American Episcopal Conference (1968) in Medellín, Colombia. The two conferences, which Gutiérrez attended as a theological consultant, sought to guide the Catholic Church in a comprehensive response to a globalizing and modern world.

The Church had already started down this road in the 1930s. But the horrors of World War II and the onset of the Cold War and decolonization presented new challenges for a faith growing rapidly in a colonized Latin America and the "mission territories" of Africa and Asia. Places and people that had, until then, been mere afterthoughts in the halls of Rome now held the key to Catholicism's future in the modern world. In a 1962 radio address on the eve of the second council, Pope John XXIII argued for the Church to present itself to the "underdeveloped countries" as "Church of all, and especially the Church of the poor."

Chile's Manuel Larraín Errazuriz, from Talca, and Brazil's Dom Hélder Câmara, from Rio, would pick up the Pope's call. The two bishops helped organize the informal Domus Mariae group, representing a two-thirds voting majority of Latin American bishops, that successfully organized bishops to approve liturgical and interfaith reforms rather than simply rubber-stamp the previous Vatican Council of 1870. At the same time, French theologian Paul Gauthier's *Christ, the Church and the Poor* (1963), which argued that a globalizing Church needed to address global poverty, started making the rounds in a subgroup of bishops, led by Gauthier, that called themselves the "Church of the Poor" and sought to put poverty on the agenda of the Council.

Chief among this second group of bishops was Bologna's Cardinal Giacomo Lercaro. At the end of the first session of the Second Council in 1962, Lercaro warned that "Our spirit will not be sufficiently responsive to God's design and man's expectation unless we place the Mystery of Christ . . . and the preaching of the Gospel to the poor" at the heart of the council's work. To do so, he proposed that the Church build fewer gilded churches, wear less fine red linen, and take off the multi-jeweled papal tiara, as it were. The liturgical changes sought (and eventually won) at the Council would ideally signal a more profound shift toward massing most of the institution's vast resources, not just a few individuals who had taken vows of poverty, at the service of the marginalized.

But the agenda of the poor did not drive the discussion at that council, nor at any of the subsequent ones. (In fact, Lercaro retired amid political controversy.) Despite reformers' best efforts, the economic needs of the global majority were never objects of great concern. Nevertheless, the Church of the Poor reaffirmed its commitment in a "Catacombs Pact," signed in 1965 primarily by up-and-coming Latin American bishops but also by lesser-known North Atlantic and Asian-stationed prelates, vowing to implement a vision of simplicity and service to the poor upon returning home.

Taking stock of these developments a decade later, Gutiérrez expressed disillusionment about global institutions' attempts at economic development in Latin America. The largesse of the Alliance for Progress, a U.S. development financing program responding to the Cuban Revolution, had not borne fruit, and the Church hierarchy was moving too slowly. Reaching the poor was an urgent matter of faith, Gutiérrez thought, not just politics. By 1970, five years after the Second Council closed, 349 million of the world's 654 million Catholics lived in the Global South, and some 256 million lived in Latin America—where 40 percent of the population lived below the poverty line.

The 1965 *Gaudium et Spes*, one of the Council's main documents, had allowed besieged populations—those "oppressed by a public authority overstepping its competence"—to "defend their own rights and the rights of their fellow citizens against the abuse of this authority." In "Populorum Progressio" (1966), John's successor, Pope Paul VI, nodded to the alleged positive benefits of colonialism and condemned revolutionary violence but—perhaps regretting some of those statements—would go on to bless African decolonization in 1967. How could one not have seen revolutionary violence as a legitimate (though certainly not the only) response to glacial progress?

At that point, Latin American bishops realized that advancing a theology suitable for their countries' poor was a task they would have to take on themselves. The Second Latin American Episcopal Conference, where Gutiérrez served on various commissions, made significant progress toward this end. Câmara, now in Recife, Brazil, had already argued the need to combat inequality in a 1966 preparatory conference in Argentina. Working with social movements in pursuit of goals such as agrarian reform and labor rights, he argued, would prove that religion was not merely an opiate of the people. The bishops at the Medellín conference laid out what they saw as some of Latin America's harsh realities—economic and political dependency on the North Atlantic countries, the need for rapid urbanization, high illiteracy, and a weak internal productive capacity and market—and they called on governments to develop policies to address them.

Gutiérrez also wrote in the midst of the dictatorial backlash against the Cuban Revolution and Richard Nixon's increasing concern about socially active priests in Latin America and the Caribbean. Though Nixon wanted to blame radicals for upsetting the stability of the social order, the U.S. State Department was clear-eyed about the threats of inaction. Though "the forces arrayed against the progressives and church-sponsored social reform . . . remain impressive," intelligence analysts wrote, and "the conservative establishments that control most of the countries are much stronger than the proponents of change," this state of affairs was far from permanent. These forces might keep revolution in check in the short term, but eventually "frustration over lack of progress, in fact, may lead progressive and radical churchmen into becoming an increasingly disruptive force both within the church and in Latin America in general." Such warnings proved more than prophetic. They directly guided U.S. policy, which sought to discredit socially minded elements of the Catholic Church as hopelessly in thrall to communism.

Indeed, Gutiérrez's choice to dedicate his book to José María Arguedas and Antônio Henrique Pereira Neto speaks to the region's perilous political and religious conflicts—and to the growing sense of a Latin American political and ethnic identity they crystallized. The work of Arguedas, a Peruvian poet and personal friend of Gutiérrez's, contrasted Andean Indigenous cosmologies with Western materialism, manifest in both traditional colonization and orthodox Marxist materialism. Neto, a young sociologist and priest who worked with Câmara in Recife, was murdered in 1969 under Brazil's new military regime.

And if economic progress was measured by national autonomy, Latin America's situation was also grim. In 1950 Argentine economist Raúl Prebisch had warned that "the enormous benefits that derive from increased productivity have not reached the periphery in a measure comparable to that obtained by the peoples of the great industrial countries." Even after the 1950s and 1960s, when Brazil and Mexico had achieved their industrialization targets, the situation had simply deteriorated further.

It was this context that led Gutiérrez to reject "a spiritual life removed from worldly concerns." Communion with God, he insisted, should mean addressing the failure of development and the persistence of abject poverty. If, as Antonio Gramsci argued, philosophy was for everyone, so, for Gutiérrez, was theology. Christians could and should become "organic intellectuals" by prophetically denouncing injustice and announcing the Good News of a society to come here on earth. Like Augustine, Gutiérrez argued that Christians should interpret the changing times in light of Scripture's historical and future-oriented visions to discern where God stood.

Discerning a path forward from the 1970s realities was even more important given the coexistence of Marxist and Christian worldviews in Latin America, both of which offered egalitarian views of the future. Gutiérrez made clear that Christianity and Marxism had important differences, though these differences, for him, led to "direct and fruitful confrontation" rather than irreconcilable conflict. Through this debate, Christianity would have to search "for its own sources" to better understand both the role of humans in history and how to transform the world.

Developmental theorists such as Joseph A. Schumpeter, Colin Clark, and François Perroux had offered one answer. They argued that economic development could both serve the common good and foster innovation. The newly independent Asian and African countries that met at the 1955 Bandung Conference had also demanded a right to economic development as opposed to a cycle of debt with industrialized colonial powers. It encouraged its participants to sell finished goods instead of raw materials.

The failure of this path led younger social scientists such as Enzo Faletto and Fernando Henrique Cardoso (who would later serve as Brazil's president), Theotonio dos Santos, and Andre Gunder Frank to focus less on the stages of development of individual economies and societies than on their position in the global economic system. Under these new theories, countries were either "peripheral" or "central," dependent on others or in a position to profit from dependence. It was here, Gutiérrez thought, that theology could enter into the fold. If dependency was a form of domination or oppression, did Christians not have the obligation to take up the struggle to liberate the region from it?

A THEOLOGY OF LIBERATION's sweeping review of 1970s Latin America, development, and dependency theories can sometimes lead one to forget that it is primarily a theological work. Yes, those who shared "the same political option" were often "Christians of different confessions . . . often marginal to their respective ecclesiastical authorities," Gutiérrez wrote. But this diversity should not water down Christianity for the sake of cooperation, he thought. It should instead cause these Christians to ponder what their faith as such could contribute to conflictual or postrevolutionary societies.

At the heart of Gutiérrez's own theology lay a "qualitative" view of salvation. Gutiérrez, like the Second Council, rejected an overspiritualizing of the Jewish prophets rooted in Blaise Pascal's anti-Semitic reading of the Tanakh as merely a precursor to the New Testament. The Tanakh contained forceful denunciations of economic inequalities, but some Christian philosophers like Pascal had argued these could be ignored altogether as if it was simply a Jewish "carnal" precursor to the "true" heavenly salvation.

If followers were freed of this misreading, Gutiérrez argues, they would find that Christian beliefs had liberatory implications in the present. "By his death and resurrection, he redeems us from sin and all its consequences," he writes. Salvation was not merely "a cure for sin in this life" but rather a "communion of human beings with God and among themselves," wrestling with "all human reality" and transforming it "to its fullness in Christ." In a break from traditional North Atlantic theologians, Gutiérrez suggests that salvation required denunciation—what Herbert Marcuse called a "great refusal" of current social arrangements. But it could not stay there. A society in the fullness of Christ would achieve utopia, the "city of the future" envisioned by Thomas More where "the common good prevails, where there is no private property, no money or privileges." Quoting Che

Guevara, Gutiérrez points out such a society would not simply have "shining factories." Rather, it was "intended to help the whole person." "Human beings," Che thought, "must be transformed."

This vision had both social and theological implications. The Kingdom could not be reduced only to "temporal progress," or the improvement of material conditions—an error Gutiérrez claimed even the Council and Teilhard de Chardin had made. Sin, "the fundamental obstacle to the Kingdom," was "also the root of all misery and injustice." The Christian must accept not only personal salvation but "the liberating gift of Christ" embodied in "all struggle against exploitation and alienation." The Church as an institution also had an obligation to speak out. "Its denunciation must be public," Gutiérrez concluded, "for its position in Latin American society is public."

The Exodus story is the "paradigmatic" lens through which Gutiérrez reads this salvation history. God desires the liberation of his people, but even they can look back fondly on "the security of slavery" by "beginning to forget" the horrors of enslavement in Egypt, Gutiérrez writes. But the very act of breaking free of Pharaoh's grip leads to a "desacralization" of the prevailing social order and justifies direct Christian action in history. If there is any "final meaning of history," such an end gives "value to the present." God's promise of salvation in the future should drive Christians to commit to a just social order now.

The most controversial section of *A Theology of Liberation* addresses the universal call of Christian love in a region split into oppressive and oppressed classes. Gutiérrez argues that the God of the Exodus story took sides and that Christians must as well. Quoting the French bishops, he points out that class struggles were a fact, not something one advocated or deplored. More importantly, as Brazilian educator Paulo Freire argued in *Pedagogy of the Oppressed* (1968), liberating the oppressed would liberate the oppressors as well. "One loves the oppressors by liberating them from their inhuman condition as oppressors," Gutiérrez writes—that is, "by liberating them from themselves." Quoting Che again, he emphasizes revolution as an act of love in a Latin American context. While in the 1988 edition Gutiérrez was careful to denounce "terrorism and repression," in the original text he was more ambiguous. "The political arena is necessarily conflictual," he had written. "The building of a just society means the confrontation—in which different kinds of violence are present—between groups with different interests and opinions." In short, violence was natural in the pursuit of liberation, even if one should do all one could to avoid it.

These ideas presaged a convergence between North Atlantic and Latin American liberation theologies. In the United States, Black American theologian James H. Cone was already making similar arguments in response to the civil rights movement's turn toward Black Power. "Unless the empirical denominational church makes a determined effort to recapture the man Jesus through a total identification with the suffering poor as expressed in Black Power," Cone wrote in *Black Theology and Black Power* in 1969, "that church will become exactly what Christ is not." Cone also prefigured Freire, who would later write in the foreword to the 1986 edition of Cone's book, *A Black Theology of Liberation*: "The man who enslaves another enslaves himself. . . . Whites are thus enslaved to their own egos.

Therefore, when blacks assert their freedom in self-determination, whites too are liberated."

GUTIÉRREZ'S BOOK had limited reach in the English-speaking world until its 1973 translation, which generated immediate commentary. His seeming endorsement of violence caused concern among mainstream U.S. theologians distant from harsh Latin American realities. Paul Schilling, writing in *The Thomist*, chided Gutiérrez for an alleged lack of ethical analysis: "One misses in this perceptive interpretation any critical examination of the role of revolutionary violence from the standpoint of Christian ethics." A 1975 *National Catholic Reporter* article covering a transnational liberation theology conference in Detroit saw support for violence as a prophetic contradiction in Gutiérrez's thought. "A Christian can employ violence when it is the lesser of existing evils," the article contends. "Instead of Isaiah's exhortation to turn swords into plowshares, liberation theology would turn altar rails into barricades."

Gutiérrez's reception in the Global South and nonwhite America was quite different. In 1971 the *National Catholic Reporter* highlighted a conference he headlined with Puerto Rican independence movements, the North American Congress on Latin America (NACLA), and Mexican American priests like Father Ralph Ruiz, who had worked to bring the plight of the hungry and poor in San Antonio to the national stage. The book received its share of critiques from these other audiences, but they were generative. Authors such as

Native American theologian and activist Vine Deloria Jr. criticized the entire category of liberation as a Western construct flattening the specific national identities of first peoples. From this perspective, liberation was not an international struggle of a universal worker subject; it was the right to the recognition of their own sovereignty, language, and difference, even if that meant drawing on their own traditions where the Old Testament failed them.

Moreover, feminists such as Mexican reproductive health scholar Itziar Lozano challenged bishops and theologians at the 1979 Puebla Conference to go beyond classifying women simply under the category of "poor." This presaged later challenges even to the very use of the Exodus story itself in Native American and Palestinian contexts. Black and African theologies, too, were conflicted over the proper balance between politics and theology, hope and anger. But for all their differences, they revolved around the revolutionary method *A Theology of Liberation* had cemented: reading scripture through the lens of liberation. It was an endlessly flexible method, this reception showed—one that could serve constituents from lesbians and women in the home to democratic resistors in Korea and caste outcasts in India.

Of course, this uptake alarmed the religious and political powers of the day. John Paul II, the Polish pope who had supported worker-priests in Europe, turned against the guiding philosophy of those who had put him over the top in his 1978 election. The CIA developed informal plans to limit the reach of socially minded clergy and issued worried reports about their progress. Well-heeled Catholic libertarians like Novak wrote polemics. Local governments killed

U.S. Catholic women missionaries in El Salvador—eliciting only silence from the Reagan administration. The Vatican's Congregation for the Doctrine of the Faith took aim at liberation theologies for replacing the Kingdom of God with revolution, importing heretical theories from Europe in the name of local theology, and calling for the dismantling of the Church hierarchy. Gutiérrez himself narrowly avoided censure by a tie vote of his own country's conference of bishops.

In the 1988 edition of *A Theology of Liberation*, Gutiérrez responded both to critiques of the book and to the crackdown on the broader movement. He astutely updated the work in various ways. He cited John Paul II's more favorable encyclicals on the working class, declared dependency theory obsolete, and reflected the growth in feminist and identity-based theologies, which drew attention to the "doubly oppressed and marginalized." He referenced the Brazilian bishops' wrestling with the country's continuing injustices during their Abolition Centennial. And in a completely rewritten section, he highlighted racism in South Africa and acknowledged ongoing conflicts in "Northern Ireland, Poland, Guatemala, and Korea"—and changed "class struggle" to the more anodyne "social conflict." But he also framed the project of liberation as largely a success. In this, he rejected the claim of conservative Catholics that the movement had driven the faithful into Latin American evangelicalism.

Demographics were not everything. Gutiérrez's thought has continued to inform social movements both within Latin America and around the world. It instilled courage in figures such as the martyred Óscar Romero, canonized as a saint in 2018, and Argentina's Enrique Angelelli, declared a martyr that same year. In 1975 Paul VI praised liberation theology's ecclesial base communities as "a hope for the universal Church." The late global health advocate Paul Farmer took inspiration from Gutiérrez. Even a mainstay of the Catholic hierarchy's opposition to reforms, German bishop Gerhard Müller, published a book with Gutiérrez in 2015.

Liberation theology's influence further manifests in the long-running debate among Latin American evangelicals about the role of social justice and liberation. While recent political trends have underscored evangelicals' focus on conservative cultural values, among a substantial minority of evangelical intellectuals and a significant part of working-class evangelicals in countries like Brazil there remains a healthy respect for implementing public policies reflecting the values the liberationists advocated.

Gutiérrez was not the first theologian to write about liberation, nor did his book provide the most expansive definition of the movement. But it might have been the most politically instrumental: here was a work that both responded to the specific context of 1970s Latin America and foresaw our changing politics of recognition more broadly. In the 1990s, beaten down by harsh political repression and socialism's apparent discrediting after 1989, the liberation theology school seemed, for a moment, to have finally run out of steam. But it never fully died. How could it? Gutiérrez's simple message—that God is on the side of the poor and marginalized—is one forever waiting to be retooled for shifting times.

FREEDOM FROM FAMILY
Will Holub-Moorman

IN 1965 Daniel Patrick Moynihan, a political scientist then serving as an assistant secretary of labor for Lyndon B. Johnson, wrote a report titled "The Negro Family: A Case for National Action." Over seventy pages, the document argued that a rising number of Black families headed by single mothers was an obstacle to Black equality, blaming disproportionate rates of marital dissolution and out-of-wedlock births on a cultural "tangle of pathology" inflicted by slavery and racism.

Moynihan thought this analysis was essential to effective anti-racist and antipoverty policy because it showed why civil and voting rights legislation were not enough. Many critics saw it differently, accusing the report of emboldening right-wing racism by "blaming the victim." Moynihan would later write that the "bloody nose" he got scared other liberals away from critically examining family structure.

That reluctance did not last. By the mid-1980s, "broken families" were once again being blamed for intergenerational "dependency," and Moynihan, now a U.S. senator, felt it was time to speak on the subject again. The result was a series of lectures at Harvard, later published as *Family and Nation* (1986), in which Moynihan cast himself as an unfairly maligned prophet of family decline whose ideas were being twisted into fodder for Ronald Reagan's assault on the welfare state. The sheer prevalence and acceleration of family breakdown made it no longer primarily a matter of racial inequality but a national crisis, Moynihan argued. He exhorted liberals to acknowledge that "poverty is now inextricably associated with family structure" and to unite behind a suite of policies: "family preservation" and youth job programs, a national family allowance, and toughened child support enforcement. The aim, as Moynihan envisioned it, was both to reclaim the nuclear family as a source of economic opportunity and to contest the conservative lie that welfare programs themselves were responsible for family breakdown.

This liberal politics of the family has proven enormously influential. Moynihan's blend of demographic alarmism and technocratic optimism was quickly amplified by a cohort of social scientists shuffling between academia, government working groups, and centrist think tanks in the 1980s and '90s. Their staunch arguments that welfare policy could encourage family formation, the historian Alice O'Connor has shown, played a key role in shaping and rallying bipartisan support for the welfare reform laws that swept the United States in the 1980s and '90s—laws that still structure U.S. family governance. Many of these figures came to oppose the punitive aspects of such legislation. But, like Moynihan, they took all this as evidence that the United States had yet to implement a truly pro-family national policy. By 2008, presidential candidate Barack Obama was campaigning on the claim that "more than half of all black children live in single-parent households ... and the foundations of our community are weaker for it."

The entrenchment of these views at the highest levels of Democratic policymaking has made a certain narrow concern for the two-parent family a centerpiece of the liberal political imagination. As sociologist Melinda Cooper has shown, this politics of the family came to focus more on policing kinship responsibilities among poor Americans than on rebuilding a family-centric economy. Along the way, liberal policymakers and scholars began to talk about the two-parent family structure principally as a model of private economic duty to be imposed on undisciplined parents, downplaying its status as a historically contingent social structure for organizing care labor and child-rearing.

On the other side of decades of liberal family policy, we can clearly see two fundamental problems with this outlook. First, it ignores demographic realities. Downward trends in marriage and dual parenthood have endured, especially for the poorest Americans, *despite* the punitive welfare and child support systems built in the name of combating them. (The United States is not alone: nearly every OECD country has seen declining marriage rates over the past few decades.) Among other things, this disjuncture of policy and reality reinforces racial inequalities through disparate exposure to the punitive family law system. Second, this outlook stifles scrutiny of the family as a lived social structure. If the state has done its duty in promoting familial responsibility, why worry about race- and class-based disparities? Why ask whether children are thriving inside and outside of family life? Why wonder whether there are better ways to organize how we raise children, live together, and care for each other?

Two recent books—*The Two-Parent Privilege* by economist Melissa Kearney and *Family Abolition* by social theorist M. E. O'Brien—take up these deeper inquiries but wind up in opposite places, one lauding the family as a sociolegal structure and the other calling to abolish it. While the authors employ very different methods and have clearly incommensurate politics, they converge in recognizing the structural economic forces that cause families to form and collapse. Where they disagree is on whether the family form—however unrepresentative or inaccessible it has become—ought to remain the horizon of social policy.

AT FIRST BLUSH, *The Two-Parent Privilege* might seem like a rehash of the work of Kearney's late twentieth-century forebears. A professor at the University of Maryland, she holds posts at some of the premier institutions of technocratic centrism, including the Aspen Economic Strategy Group, MIT's Poverty Action Lab, and the Brookings Institution (the last of which was a key booster of research on family structure in the 1980s and '90s).

There are certainly resemblances between Kearney's work and her predecessors'. The central claim of *The Two-Parent Privilege*—that, all else equal, children raised in the United States by single parents fare significantly worse economically than those raised by married parents—has been conventional wisdom in establishment social

Holub-Moorman

thought for so long that few have bothered to try to prove it. (There is a difference between "two-parent" and "married" households, of course, but for Kearney they collapse in practice, given "the fairly low rate of unmarried parental cohabitation in the United States.") Like earlier work in this vein, the book repeatedly invokes "upward mobility"—what it clearly sees as the essence of social equality—while ignoring its relationship to *downward* mobility. And like other post-Moynihan scholars, Kearney intends to steer clear of culturalist explanations or judgments. "I am not blaming single mothers," she insists. "I am not diminishing the pernicious effects of racism in the United States."

What sets Kearney's vision apart from her forebears' is that she lacks their faith that social policy can reverse the trend to single parenthood. Although she thinks it would be a good thing if more children experienced the "two-parent privilege," she argues that government has proven unable to guarantee it—especially since the economic restructurings of the 1970s, and especially for poor children. As the book points out, the rate of children living with married parents in the United States has fallen from 77 percent in 1980 to 63 percent in 2019; most of the drop is among working-class Americans. While the state should not entirely give up on promoting dual parenthood, Kearney concludes, it should focus more on mitigating the economic effects of the parenting gap through a sort of Pigouvian subsidy: expanding welfare benefits and child tax credits for both one- and two-parent poor families, as well as investing in early-childhood public education. (Universal child care is notably absent from Kearney's vision, perhaps reflecting a belief in the irreplaceable value of *parental* care.) If these provisions end up allowing more families to form or stay together, Kearney thinks, so much the better.

Kearney defines the "two-parent privilege" in terms of economic outcomes. On the basis of longitudinal studies, she argues that children in two-parent homes receive more care, attention, and intellectual stimulation than those raised by single parents—and that this difference affects their later educational performance, job prospects, earnings, and so on. The reason is not that single parents are bad parents, Kearney argues, but simply that they tend to have less time, emotional bandwidth, and flexibility in organizing caregiving duties than two-parent families. Furthermore, she maintains, given that the vast majority of single parents are single mothers, the absence of men in families has a negative impact on the emotional development of boys in particular. A crucial data point for Kearney is the fact that unequal economic and educational outcomes are not reducible to income disparities between single-parent and two-parent homes. The physical presence of an extra parent makes a key difference.

Kearney's skepticism about the state's ability to promote dual parenthood arises from her diagnosis of declining marriage rates, which she attributes to the declining economic position of non-college-educated men over the past several decades. Deindustrialization, the pay-productivity gap, union decline, and mass incarceration have all contributed to a general decrease in what Kearney, following sociologist William Julius Wilson, calls the "marriageability" of working-class men. Since 1980, she writes, "among workers without a four-year college degree, the gap between men's earnings

Holub-Moorman

and women's earnings shrank considerably (on account of both increasing earnings among women and stagnant earnings among men), which lessened the economic incentive (and imperative) for some women to marry."

Other authors, it should be noted, have long pursued this line of reasoning into deeply antifeminist territory, arguing variously that women's efforts to gain an equal wage with men and expand their vocational options have upset a natural hierarchy of gender relations and helped normalize low-waged and precarious jobs. Kearney tries to assure readers that her causal models of marriage and child-rearing simply *reflect* rather than *endorse* a heteronormative division of labor. But these gestures are somewhat too perfunctory to carry much force.

Indeed, *The Two-Parent Privilege* views the prospect of restoring marriage rates by reinstalling the male breadwinner less as an ideological or ethical nonstarter than as a practical impossibility. In one of the book's most revealing sections, Kearney discusses a recent study of hers which finds that "improvements in the economic prospects of less educated men have not been shown . . . to usher in an increase in marriage and married-parent families." In a Moynihanian move, Kearney concludes that growing rates of single parenthood over the past few decades have gradually produced a "new social paradigm" that is mysteriously resistant to economic incentives to marry. Socially conservative scholars have interpreted this study as support for their broader claims that "hookup culture," accessible contraception, and online pornography have encouraged the cultural decline of marriage. Kearney does not follow them into blaming sexual liberalization, but she admits that "reversing recent trends in family structure will likely require both economic *and* social changes." However shrewdly, she does not speculate about what social changes would do the trick.

It is to the book's credit that it has very little patience for the "new paternalist" contrivances embraced by late twentieth-century welfare reformers. There just isn't any evidence, Kearney rightly notes, to support the idea that cutting single parents' benefits and hunting down absent ones has meaningfully encouraged the formation and maintenance of two-parent homes. Nor does the book call for or lend any direct support to recent conservative calls to rescind no-fault divorce laws and promote covenant marriages. Kearney sees some room for growth in local programs encouraging involved fatherhood, but she treats them as more likely to improve outcomes for children than to promote marriage stability. What scholar Gilbert Steiner bemoaned over forty years ago as the "futility of family policy" in solving the problems of American families re-emerges here as a central takeaway of Kearney's book.

Critics of *The Two-Parent Privilege* might take one of two broad tacks. One is methodological: asking whether Kearney's model is really an accurate depiction of socioeconomic reality when it comes to marriage and child-rearing. There are plenty of analytical moves and omissions one might object to. For example, Kearney admits that "it is possible that mothers who raise children on their own are able to compensate for the lack of another adult in the home, perhaps with their own resources or the help of a network of family and friends," but she doesn't discuss the

Holub-Moorman

possibility further. Nor does she devote much attention to the actual lives and decisions of single parents, which might have enriched her causal models.

Others might doubt that the number crunching means what Kearney says it does. Matt Bruenig, for example, notes that comparing married and unmarried couples—even when controlling for race and class—cannot be used to estimate the causal effect of marriage on children's outcomes for any *particular* set of parents, because nonmarital status is closely correlated with relationship dysfunction (which isn't measured in Kearney's dataset). For this reason, it does not follow that every pair of working-class parents could boost their children's economic fortunes simply by getting married. Though Kearney acknowledges that there are situations in which marriage would not be beneficial or would even be harmful for parents and their children, she does not address the broader implications of this methodological critique for her findings.

But regardless of these concerns, there is a more fundamental objection. It is possible to agree that "two-parent privilege" exists and drives intergenerational inequality *under our current economic system* without sharing Kearney's presumption that its institutions and organization must more or less be taken for granted. Looking at her statistical picture, one could easily conclude not that too few adults are getting married, or that too few kids are being raised in two-parent homes, but that people who adopt other models of care and commitment are systematically disadvantaged by our socioeconomic system. In this sense, the book's pessimism about putting the family back together again reveals the limits of Kearney's political imagination. Where she holds the system constant and asks how to make the best of it, others would reverse the moral: if our economic system cannot be made to sustain the very structures of social reproduction it makes essential to human flourishing, then we need new structures, or a new system.

OR BOTH, M. E. O'Brien argues in *Family Abolition: Capitalism and the Communizing of Care*. A sharp and timely synthesis of past and present anticapitalist critiques of the family, the book builds on O'Brien's earlier speculative fiction by imagining the future of care in a communist society. We need to envision such alternatives, she argues, because the private household is the stalking-horse of class society, white supremacy, and patriarchy.

One of the many admirable qualities of O'Brien's book is its reconstruction of the long history of family abolitionist thought. Although anti-family theory and practice certainly extend beyond the self-identified political left—within religious communes, for example—O'Brien focuses on those who have seen it as a key element in the overthrow of capitalism. Tracing family abolitionism from early nineteenth-century calls to dismantle the bourgeois family (which Marx and Engels sportively dubbed the "infamous proposal of the Communists"), through the revolutionary moments of the Paris Commune and the early Soviet Union, and then into the "Red Decade" of radical feminism and gay liberation between the mid-1960s and '70s, the book's middle section carefully charts how condemnations of the family form and socialist thought evolved alongside each other—even if not always harmoniously, as evident in conflicts between leftist family abolitionists and the industrial workers' movement over the breadwinner family form.

O'Brien's overriding focus on dismantling the private household—the legal-economic form of the family as a "unit of privatized care"—sets her book slightly apart from the work of other contemporary family abolitionists. Family violence is totally missing from Kearney's book, but it is a central concern of O'Brien's. Much of it, she argues, is enabled and obscured by the fact that its victims feel—often correctly—that leaving families would sacrifice their primary source of care and economic security, or even expose them to further violence. "The family as a social form joins together care and coercion, dependency and love, abuse and affection," she writes, and our society's laws and lack of a meaningful welfare state encourage people not only to accept but to idealize this compromise. Queer youth whose parents don't accept them know all too well what they stand to lose if they are cut off from the "privilege" Kearney identifies—as do the many people who remain in abusive or unhappy marriages for the sake of their children.

Unlike Kearney, O'Brien views the decline in marriage and rise in single parenthood as a "huge improvement in human freedom," but she cautions against being too sanguine about these shifts. For many working-class women, she notes, financial domination by a husband has simply been exchanged for the "impersonal domination" of wage labor, liberation from certain forms of violence coming at the cost of new forms of exploitation and risk. Meanwhile, she notes, this decline has not undermined the ideological force and seductiveness of the family for both conservatives and social democrats: it still serves as the basis for assaults on reproductive rights and public education, as well as the spread of the "family policing system" of child protective services and state bans on gender-affirming care for minors.

What should be done? In recent years, legal scholars such as Nancy Polikoff and John Culhane have argued that declining marriage rates, along with the expanding state recognition of non-heterosexual relationships, show it is long past time to decouple state-provided rights, benefits, and obligations from marital status. O'Brien takes such ideas seriously, devoting an entire chapter to "progressive anti-family reforms" such as universal welfare benefits and aligning law with the social reality of familial relationships. To the extent that state policy can reduce the advantages gained by forming a private household and the burdens incurred by leaving one, she argues, it is worth pursuing. But O'Brien also sees real dangers in pursuing family abolition through the state. She points to welfare's "dehumanizing" and invasive past, as well as the risk that an overweening government wields its power to delegitimize nontraditional kinship and "chosen family" relationships among historically marginalized groups.

It is here that O'Brien departs most clearly from prior left-feminist critiques of the family. Earlier thinkers such as Soviet feminist Alexandra Kollontai and radical feminist Shulamith Firestone thought that women's oppression would never end without disrupting the mother-child bond. For Kollontai, this meant the socialist state's near-total assumption of child-rearing duties; for Firestone, the erosion of gendered labor through mass cybernation and reliance on artifi-

Holub-Moorman

cial reproduction. O'Brien's vision is instead voluntaristic, unfolding through individual choices and collective experiments freed from the primarily economic compulsions of the family. As she puts it, family abolition means "the destruction of private households as systems of accumulating power and property at the cost of others' well-being" but "not the destruction of kinship ties that currently serve as protection against white supremacy, poverty, and state violence."

On this point, O'Brien is clearly echoing critiques of family abolitionist thought by feminists of color. As Hazel Carby and others have argued, attacks on the family have tended to ignore—or even pathologize—family and kinship ties among marginalized groups as a source of resistance, solidarity, and pleasure. Toward the outset of her book, O'Brien tries to square this circle by arguing that the social relations called "families" in oppressed groups often "do not quite constitute a private household as a unit of privatized care." They are therefore not recognized as families by "dominant social institutions," and for that reason they are not the target of her critique.

But this distinction misses some of the radical edge of other anti-family arguments. Despite her background as a psychoanalyst, O'Brien has relatively little to say about what familial child-rearing does to children's identities and attitudes (or to parents' for that matter), beyond a few passages highlighting the family as the primary enforcer of "alienated gender expectations" and heteronormativity. (This family-cultivated alienation might not be limited to gender identity, some midcentury Freudo-Marxists argued; it could extend to complexes of deference and docility that "operate to maintain the stability of class society," as Erich Fromm put it.) Nor does she reflect more than passingly on earlier left-feminists' charge that the family is inherently "anti-social" because it unjustly privileges kinship over other forms of social connection. This marks a divergence between *Family Abolition* and another recent communist manifesto, Sophie Lewis's *Abolish the Family* (2022), which takes aim at not just the economic coercion of the capitalist family but the "uncomradely hierarchy" baked into even the most radical manifestations of kinship such as the "chosen family."

O'Brien's vision takes firmer shape in her book's closing chapters, which speculate on communal life in the aftermath of anticapitalist revolution. Blending the utopian socialism of Charles Fourier with the left-communist ideas associated with *Endnotes* and The Invisible Committee, O'Brien envisions a stateless landscape populated by self-governing communes of a few hundred people. Within these communes, she suggests that forms of care and parenting would be intentionally heterogeneous, fluid, and voluntary: people could choose to raise their biological children in "family-like arrangements," or turn them over to the care of crèches, or something in between, with no expectation of permanence. Children would be empowered to leave or join living situations according to their desires.

O'Brien is emphatic that these associations be voluntary. "It does not require a romantic idealization of the mother-child bond," she writes, "to recognize that the experience of conception and gestation can often lead to an emotional tie, and that universally severing this tie could be a form of injustice." The looming question is whether there is something like a "natural" basis for the nuclear family as an arrangement of care—as its defenders have so often

Holub-Moorman

claimed—and, if so, whether it justifies sharp limits on coercing people out of families in the name of the social good (or even individual well-being).

Consider a child whose biological parents are members of a religious sect that emphasizes the divine quality of patriarchal domination and practices self-imposed exclusion from society writ large. Should a society with feminist commitments respect this family arrangement, even if being raised by these parents makes it overwhelmingly likely that the child will not "choose" to leave and will opt to become a member of the sect—thereby reproducing patriarchy? In the interests of not "reproducing the imperialist violence of a white liberalism that seeks to 'save' anyone against their will," O'Brien says yes—"conditioned on . . . allowing outside contact for all residents, giving women, queers, or others experiencing oppression a chance to encounter and choose the outside world."

One challenge for this view—as O'Brien acknowledges—is that oppression is often not subjectively experienced or recognized as such, particularly in the context of the family. As Lauren Berlant put it in *Cruel Optimism* (2011), for many people "the promise of familial love is the conveyance for the incitement to misrecognize the bad life as a good one." O'Brien is compelled by the idea that eliminating the family's economic function will tend to demystify these relations and allow people to choose the kind of care—the kind of life—that is in some sense best for them. Readers more suspicious of the affective hold of the family will want a more direct or even aggressive strategy to dismantle the injustice they see in the present. But regardless of what side one comes down on, *Family Abolition* offers a compelling provocation to think about the possibilities of human freedom in a post-family world, and how we might achieve them.

ALTHOUGH THEIR political lexicons, goals, and likely audiences could not be more different, both *The Two-Parent Privilege* and *Family Abolition* acknowledge that the family is not fulfilling the tasks of social reproduction that have been delegated to it, that protracted shifts in political economy are the culprit, and that nudges or tweaks to incentives can't help. Together they offer a strong tonic for the fantasy that the two-parent family can be put back together through top-down welfare and tax policy, which is once again a cause célèbre of the more technocratic tendencies within contemporary social conservatism.

At the same time, the decline of marriage and the two-parent family does not necessarily mean that society is becoming less familial. The family form has survived and adapted in response to previous crises of capitalism, assuming different shapes while continuing to facilitate the privatized distribution of wealth and care. This does not demand a set number of biological parents in the home; it only requires that people channel their energy, resources, identities, and commitments in the service of economic units bound by kinship.

"Families tend to hide the very existence of common interests by training people to consider that their worries are personal and

Holub-Moorman

private, when in fact they are social," historian Linda Gordon wrote in 1970. A half-century of jeremiads about family breakdown from Moynihan and his successors notwithstanding, they still do. Even if more children are now growing up with fewer parents than Kearney deems ideal—or are living in arrangements that don't constitute a private household as O'Brien understands it—they still learn to invest in kinship in a way that may deepen the more essentially it serves to protect them against precarity.

As a theoretical tradition, anti-family critique can and should point out how the family currently reproduces an unjust economic system and oppresses those who cannot access its idealized form. At the same time, it should not shy away from demystifying the psychic claims of kinship. This does not mean shaming or stigmatizing those who love their families, but it does mean showing why familial love comes with burdens that we need not be collectively doomed to bear.

WHAT DOES IT MEAN TO BE FREE?

Nathalie Etoke interviewed by Lewis Gordon

NATHALIE ETOKE's *Black Existential Freedom* (2022) begins with a challenge. "Does the continuous destruction of Black life," she asks, "invalidate the possibility of freedom?" She finds it difficult to imagine a liberatory politics arising from an "agonizing fixation on oppression." In her book, she insists there is a different path—one that can imagine collective freedom in the face of domination. To get there, she draws on the Black existentialist tradition, which carries a deep appreciation of the creative power of Black life.

In this recent conversation, which has been edited for length and clarity, Etoke and Lewis Gordon, professor of philosophy at the University of Connecticut, discuss Etoke's book, the distinctiveness of Black existentialist thought, and the necessity of asserting one's humanity in the face of dehumanization.

LEWIS GORDON: To kick things off, Nathalie, can you talk about what you are trying to say in the book?

NATHALIE ETOKE: I look at the ways we understand freedom, which is usually in political terms. But I think the question goes beyond what I call the "legality of freedom" or the issue of rights. I am also interested in this idea of the inner lives of Black people. I try to point out that if we only look—as Afropessimists do—at Black life through the lens of white supremacy or social death, in many ways we are erasing and silencing the ways Blackness has to do with an affirmation of life in the context of oppression for the sake of freedom.

Black freedom is not something that is given; it is fought for—yes, from the perspective of human rights, but also from an existential perspective. How do you define yourself in your own terms? And how do you practice existence in the context of oppression? You constantly have this tension. That's what I observed—and I've been "Black" on three different continents.

LG: So, you're Black, Black, Black.

NE: I was born in Paris, and I was raised in Cameroon. In Cameroon my racial identity didn't matter, because everybody is Black—and therefore no one is. That doesn't mean white supremacy isn't present in the education and teaching we got, but I saw other people as human beings first.

Fast forward: I moved to France, I'm eighteen and go to college—that is when I become "Black." But what does that mean? It means becoming a minority: encountering the white gaze, and also epistemic violence. I started to read Frantz Fanon in my early twenties and was struck by his writings on the burden of constantly engaging the idea that the white world has of you, which has nothing to do with who you are.

But fast forward again: I moved to the United States in July 2001, and I discovered this rich library with all these Black thinkers talking about Blackness, not just in terms of an antagonizing of yourself with the white world, but also constantly focusing on who you are—not from a narcissistic standpoint, but because you're trying to touch this freedom that at first seems too abstract and out of touch but is part of who you are, although you're excluded from it.

Take the spirituals, which are not just about God. They are about liberation and assessing your humanity, declaring that you're a child of God when people say you're not. Or look at how people talk about slavery. Often it's theorized in global, somewhat abstract, terms. But I'm interested in thinking about slavery as an experience a human being goes through. An individual who at the time knew his name, knew who he was, was somebody's mother, was somebody's father, was somebody's sister, had a language, but found himself or herself in the hold of that slave ship, unable to communicate with other people, but then realizes that, oh, all of us down here are Black. What does that mean? All these questions inform my perspective.

What makes Black existentialism very unique, I think, is this situation of despair and tragedy and ontological catastrophe that you constantly have to engage—not only from an existentialist standpoint, but in the material conditions of your life. So, when I look at the ways Black immigrants are treated, whether we're talking about Europe or America today, I ask: What is there that makes their exclusion unique?

LG: I think the Afropessimists completely distort what Fanon actually said—that "the Black man has no ontological resistance in the eyes of the white man." He is not saying that Black people lack ontological resistance at all. They confuse the title of his book. The title is *Black Skin*, which is to be sealed in your skin, and *White Masks*, which is the lie that many white people wear. In that part of the analysis, he was talking about how white people need to *believe* that Black people have no ontological resistance. That's why he said, "in the eyes of the white man." But the eyes of Black people among one another, we know we have a lot of ontological resistance, which you beautifully talk about in the book.

NE: That's why I start my book by bringing up George Floyd. I say, what's the point of talking about Black existential freedom when you're constantly bombarded with images that remind you that you're not free? What do you do with that? To me, this is the fundamental tension we need to address: that you must define the value of your life despite its being constantly devalued. You need to have another way of looking at who you are that goes beyond the dehumanization you encounter.

LG: Why Black existentialism? How does Black existentialism get at these questions?

NE: It's very simple. Black people of African descent are part of the world, but we're also excluded from it. We live in a reality that we did not create. But there we are; we have to exist. And we have to find a way to exist and be free.

Of course, this is also the human condition. You don't choose the historical and political circumstances under which you're born, no matter your racial background. But I think racism is like the icing on the cake—an unnecessary suffering that you didn't choose. And that's why I come to this idea of existence. It's like, I am out here in this world, knowing that there is a struggle, there is a fight. And it can be tiring. You can feel that it's not fair. But you're here. What are you going to do about it? This struggle is both existential and material; it is political, philosophical, economic. Many issues overlap. That's why I'm also very wary of those ontologizing Blackness, just talking about Blackness. I think we also have to talk about the material conditions of our lives.

At the end of *Black Skin, White Masks*, Fanon asks the following question: "Was my freedom not given to me then in order to build the world of the *You?*" This entails a kind of interrelationality that even transcends Blackness. How do we create a world where my existence is there to build a world with you—a relation with you? Because at the end of the day, some of the key issues in Black existentialism address this failure to connect with yourself, if you internalize racism, and also with the outside world, which really works at cutting up that connection.

I don't speak the language, but I will never forget when I found out that, in Haitian Creole, the word *nèg* does not mean

Black. It means "man." It means "human." And I was thinking, these people have something that we lost—because you know, in Haiti, you can be a *nègre blanc*. You're just a human who happens to be white. This idea that these people who were enslaved created a language where *nèg* means "human" really turned my world upside down. Once you start thinking that way about that word, and the condition of being human from that perspective, it really changes the conversation.

LG: I think that really summarizes it beautifully. It also resists reductionism. There are multiple challenges raised by the emergence of the category of Black, because a lot of the people we called Black were not historically Black—and the people we call white, they were not historically white. They became such.

But there's something else in Black existentialism that links to the question of freedom. This is what a lot of Afropessimists miss, and a lot of critics miss. The existential critique is also a critique of ontology. When you ontologize people, you turn people into things. The whole point about humanity is to transcend being things. And there are others who talk about this, like the Japanese philosopher Keiji Nishitani. Or Ali Shariati, the Iranian philosopher. You also see it in a lot of African thought. The point of all this critique is that reality is not simply about things. It's more than that.

NE: What you say about commodification is very important. Think about how we engage the issue of identity today—it's who you are, instead of the relationship you have with other people. It doesn't mean that the relationship is easy. But we need to go about building the relationship, instead of just talking about who you are from this perspective that commodifies you as a subject.

Then, this notion of freedom. The Western narrative of freedom is self-redemptive. Some people were excluded, but now they can become part of it. I think it's much more complicated than that because the rules of that freedom are colonial rules. You cannot address that freedom without discussing the dispossession of land, the genocide of Native Americans, the enslavement of people of African descent. So maybe we need to decolonize freedom to come up with something else. I think that's why Fanon is very useful when he talks about "inventivity"—what we need to create.

LG: We're talking about the question of everyday life, right? Even under conditions of enslavement, enslaved people were finding ways to live their humanity, and they found ways to experience value and joy, and assert dignity. We know that because it is by their actions that many of us are here.

NE: In my work, I talk about active subjectivity versus passive subjectivity. Passive subjectivity is like living with white people in your head—basically, defining yourself in the context of white supremacy, and internalizing a degrading image of who you are, not because it's your fault, but because you're bombarded with this idea that you're lesser than. But then you have active subjectivity, which is the ways you resist white supremacy, not necessarily because you're trying to challenge or dismantle it, but because you know you're a human being, and you're going about your life on a regular basis. Those two forces are not mutually exclusive.

LG: There are many Black people who don't have white people in our heads. What we have in our heads are our mothers, our fathers, our brothers, our sisters, our loved ones. And it's very strange that there's a tendency, particularly in academic literature, to throw Black people always into the category of the pathological, the psychotic, the neurotic. We need to get away from these very distorted, ultimately bourgeois ways of thinking about Blackness.

The fact is that most Black people do not spend a lot of our lives walking around asking ourselves, are we white enough? We don't even ask if we're Black enough. We ask stuff like: Are we going to get enough food today? How're our friends doing? How are our neighbors? Am I going to get a job? Even in the Bronx growing up, my family, my relatives, and I, we weren't running around trying to figure out if we could be like white people. We saw the beauty in one another.

NE: I think you are maybe also talking about the working class. Class informs the way we have these conversations. In the last chapter of *Black Skin, White Masks*, Fanon talks about the fact that intellectual alienation is a creation of middle-class society. He calls the middle class "a closed society in which life has no taste, in which the air is tainted, in which ideas and men are corrupt."

Also, when we talk about Afropessimism, especially in academia, just listen to the language. People talk about "Black bodies." Of course,

I understand why the focus could be on bodies—when you think about violence and police brutality, or how people respond to the physicality of Black being. But then at the same time, what happens when we shift the conversation, and instead talk about Black people? That's what I would rather do.

A related tendency is to assume there is some kind of essential Blackness. I am one of those people who absolutely reject authenticity discourses. A human being is basically not a complete notion, but an open possibility. The problem with authenticity is that what one finds is that many people are never authentic enough. It's a nowhere discourse that leads people into a form of self-asserted purity through which they ultimately begin to dominate others. And I could put my cards on the table. I see humanity as fundamentally queer, but what goes on is a project to de-queer or to close off the possibilities of humanity in such a way that people can fit into paradigms of authenticity.

The truth of the matter is that many of us don't know what in the world we are until we live and we realize those possibilities. This is a crucial element that's linked into understanding freedom.

You also have to think about the ways the idea of authenticity has been used and abused in the context of oppression and dictatorship. I study this in my work on sub-Saharan Africa. Take Mobutu Sese Seko, the former president of what is now called the Democratic Republic of the Congo. He called the country Zaire. He changed the name of the currency to the Zaire as well. People had to change their names to reject Christian names. You had to take native names. And it was all supposed to be about authenticity and about being African.

Etoke & Gordon

But when people would bring up conversations about democracy or freedom, Mobutu would say, no, we are Africans, we believe in chiefs. So, there are also ways this language about authenticity can be very repressive and reactionary in the African context. If you really think about it, postcolonial African identity has incorporated the legacy of colonial sodomy laws, whether we're talking about the Caribbean or sub-Saharan Africa. African people never sat down somewhere to decide that being gay was a crime—it was installed by their countries' respective colonial governments.

We don't even understand the ways we keep the repressive legacy of colonialism and take the lie in the name of African identity or Christianity. But all of that has to do with repressing freedom and dehumanizing the people and disciplining and controlling queer bodies, in the context of a postcolonial crisis. The queer subject becomes a scapegoat. In a very strange and tragic kind of way, homophobia creates a connection between the oppressive ruling class, the clergy, and pauperized populations, in the context of nationalism.

LG: Hear, hear. I have one last thought for you, on the relationship between freedom and violence. One of the biggest fears in any society conditioned by white supremacy is that the society will be exposed as being built upon a lie: the double standard of violence. Black people are always being asked to be nonviolent for things that white people at the snap of a finger would use violence for. We have to bear in mind that colonialism and racism, too, are ongoing systems of violence.

The problem is, if you don't question those systems, if you don't challenge them, then you're complicit with violence. But when you stand up against those systems, you are the one called violent, because that system is treated as legitimate. Fanon pointed out—and I agree with him here—that it's a waste of time to demonstrate that you're nonviolent. Do something about the violence. Otherwise, violence and dehumanization will continue.

NE: When I think about violence, I don't just think about white violence against Black people. I think about postcolonial violence and dictatorship, the type of violence African dictators inflicted on their own people to repress freedom and the lack of accountability as well. Then I think about coups d'état that keep on happening in Burkina Faso, in Mali, in Guinea, and the ways, at least from the sub-Saharan postcolonial context, that the question of violence in relation to freedom is very complicated. At first, the people are always happy to see the dictator being removed or disappear. But then they realize that there is a military police state that is also very repressive. Then you have an oligarchy and the creation of a caste system that is also very oppressive.

In the context of sub-Saharan Africa—and I'm not talking about the nationalist struggle with people like Amílcar Cabral or what happened in Algeria with the National Liberation Front, I'm talking about now—the role that violence plays in the context of freedom and oppression is really complicated. It's shifting from one oppressive government to another. And what happens when the military is in power and they're the ones who can use the violence? They use it in the name of the people, but do they actually free the people? Do they create the condition of freedom?

Etoke & Gordon

But I agree with you. The whole argument about violence is just a way of silencing freedom, because people have moral conversations about violence only when oppressed people want to free themselves. But when the powerful want to take over some other countries because of oil, or even come up with fictitious wars, they create a narrative around the violence they use to realize their interests—because they have the power to do so. It's a lie. It's also a form of bad faith. We're living a lie, but that lie becomes the truth because of violence. If you try to challenge it—if you try to break free of the lie—they will try to repress the truth. I think that's the problem we have to deal with.

UNLUCKY

poem by Hannah Liberman

A FRIEND once told me that we come into this world cast out at sea. If you're lucky, he said, you're given swim lessons, a life vest, a group to swim around you and hold your head, arms, feet when you begin to fatigue. If you're even luckier, you've landed somewhere close to the shore, where the water is still, warm and shallow. Those people rarely realize their fortune, it's all they've ever known, and they startle when one of them drowns. Drowning is something that happens to others, not to them. Because they are given the conditions to survive, the freedom to float on their backs in the sunlight or darkness, the surface just an unbroken pane of glass opening onto either side of the world.

If you're one of the unlucky ones, you're tossed out to tread open water, throw your body beneath the waves. You teach yourself how to swim, how to find others pushed toward the same fate. Sometimes you gurgle up for air and find a view that for a moment might melt the air from your throat. Then, when the water gets too choppy, too deep, you begin to sink. And there you are below the surface, exhausting yourself just trying to get back. Sinking, sucking in salt, never allowed, never given the means, to not flail and fight for air. You are absolutely and totally free from all control, yet also absolutely and positively unfree.

How can we possibly be angry when, after watching their friends and family choke and hurt and gasp and drown, those damned learn to survive, navigate below water rather than along the surface, let their bodies do what bodies are meant to do. Move, touch another, jolt, lie still, attempt love, mourn, mourn, attempt joy, mourn, try to survive. Scream. Bleed. Love. Fuck. Mourn. Mourn. Mourn. Cry out.

Imagine a world where none of us are cast out at sea. Where we are all free *to* free *to* free *to* live. How do we get there?

But he wasn't asking me.

LIBERALISM IN MOURNING
Samuel Moyn

COLD WAR LIBERALISM was a catastrophe—for liberalism. This distinct body of liberal thought says that freedom comes first, that the enemies of liberty are the first priority to confront and contain in a dangerous world, and that demanding anything more from liberalism is likely to lead to tyranny.

This set of ideas became intellectually trendsetting in the 1940s and 1950s at the outset of the Cold War, when liberals conceived of them as essential truths the free world had to preserve in a struggle against totalitarian empire. By the 1960s it had its enemies, who invented the very phrase "Cold War liberalism" to indict its domestic compromises and foreign policy mistakes. That did not stop it from being rehabilitated in the 1990s, when it was repurposed for a post-political age. A generation of public intellectuals—among them Anne Applebaum, Timothy Garton Ash, Michael Ignatieff, and Leon Wieseltier—styled themselves as successors to Cold War liberals, trumpeting the superiority of Cold War liberalism over illiberal right and left. 1989 thus ushered in the global triumph of freedom, but on Cold War liberalism's distorted terms.

Then came the election of Donald Trump in 2016, which unleashed a great war over liberalism—a polemical one, at least—and prompted yet another resurgence of Cold War liberalism's core ideas. Patrick Deneen's much-discussed assault, *Why Liberalism Failed* (2018), was met by a crop of liberal self-defenses by the likes of Francis Fukuyama, Adam Gopnik, and Mark Lilla. Organized as much against the left as the right, these defenses—almost all of them explicitly or implicitly attempted in Cold War terms—not only rang hollow; they have failed to forestall the political crisis they promised to transcend. The result has been the reversal of Cold War liberal triumph into today's mood of desperation and despair. A few right intellectuals of Deneen's ilk have continued to call for a vague "post-liberalism," the main function of which sometimes seems to be to bait Cold War liberals into reasserting their creed.

Thanks to this eternal return, Cold War liberalism still sets the fundamental terms of the liberal outlook—in spite of all the alternatives within the liberal tradition. Lost in this shuffle was how much of a betrayal of liberalism itself Cold War liberalism had been.

Perhaps no one better illustrates this chosen fate than literary critic Lionel Trilling. One of the most admired of the Cold War liberals, Trilling was also the most remorselessly self-critical. The essays he wrote in the later 1930s and 1940s established the position of *The Liberal Imagination*, his 1950 triumph that sold almost two hundred thousand copies. Alongside Trilling's 1947 novel, *The Middle of the Journey*, his essays crystallize the abandonment of the liberal cause in the name of rescuing it from illusions and immaturity.

This kind of Cold War liberalism continues to haunt liberalism even today, but Trilling was also its most pitiless critic. We now tend to think of Cold War liberalism as a political stance with familiar implications in domestic and foreign policy, defending freedom of thought against miscreants right, left, postmodern, and "woke" at home, and choosing between containment and rollback of bigger geopolitical challengers while engaging in counterinsurgency and proxy wars around the world. Yet like so many political doctrines, Cold War liberalism was as much about the self as the state or society.

In 1958 political philosopher Isaiah Berlin famously captured this liberalism's commitment to "negative liberty," freedom against interference; by contrast, Trilling's call to contain disorderly passion for the sake of austere freedom resonated with an ideology of self-control in deep tension with the notion of liberty as noninterference. While his fellow Cold War liberal Judith Shklar, a political theorist at Harvard, defined the creed as a "liberalism of fear" that committed itself above all to avoiding cruelty, Trilling thought it also entailed self-subjugation and self-policing, and he squirmed under the self-torture he recommended. His call for a self-regulated Cold War liberal persona was never complete and unambivalent: even as a damaged life led him to impose limits, he never entirely relinquished his youthful protest against unnecessary ones.

BORN IN New York City in 1905 to Polish Jewish immigrants (his father sold fur-lined coats), Trilling had been a fellow traveler of communism very briefly, from 1931 to 1933, and he was never a party member. But in some ways he never left the 1930s, and his Cold War liberalism could be read as a kind of therapy in response. As Trilling saw it, Stalinism, far from being some foreign enemy alone or even mainly, was rooted in the form of liberalism that Trilling's generation had inherited from the nineteenth century. The deepest contest for this Cold War liberal was inside.

Trilling spent the decade after 1933 in ideological transition. He and his life companion, Diana Rubin, emerged from fellow traveling, registering their first public dissent in 1934. It was thus perhaps no accident that his first form of therapy, in choosing his dissertation topic in the midst of his communist flirtation and completing it as he weaned himself from it, was the Victorian mandarinism and moralism of Matthew Arnold—who hoped to see the ascendant middle class educated in great books to ensure that civilization would not become coarse. Trilling came by his Anglophilia more honestly than most Cold War liberals who shared it. While his lineage on both sides traced back to Białystok, it was formative that both his grandmother and his mother had been born and raised in England—and adored it. Trilling was unsure how to rescue liberalism, but Arnold's brief for high culture in *Culture and Anarchy* (1869) and other writings offered a starting point.

In the book on Arnold he published in 1939, Trilling was already aware that he was indulging in nostalgia, celebrating the best that had been thought and said. He would go on to teach in Columbia's great books program for decades, but recognized that it hardly offered a credible politics on its own. On the one hand, he was amazingly open about the need for cultural elites to anticipate and guide democratization, perhaps permanently. "Democracy assumes the ability of all men to live by the intellect," he wrote. But "we surely must question with Arnold the number of those who can support the intellectual life, even in a secondary way as pupils of the great." On the other hand, Trilling understood that cultural mandarinism couldn't solve the more basic problem: liberals were perpetually shocked by their limits and opponents, not anticipating them and sometimes reinforcing their strength. Reformers acting in the name of liberalism frequently helped its enemies (read: communists) out of enthusiasm for progress. "Surely if liberalism has a single desperate weakness," Trilling explained four years later in a book on E.M. Forster,

> it is an inadequacy of imagination: liberalism is always being sur-
> prised. There is always the liberal work to do over again because hard
> upon surprise disillusionment follows and for the moment of liberal
> fatigue reaction is always ready—reaction never hopes, despairs or
> suffers amazement.

What would it take, Trilling asked, to invent a reformed liberalism that would stop being surprised by evil—a liberalism aware that people are imperfect and that utopianism makes things worse, not least by co-opting good intentions and high ideals for bad ends and violent evils?

Trilling's answer was psychoanalysis. Sigmund Freud was the greatest "master of reality," he argued, not least in his awareness of inborn aggression, with life haunted perpetually by a death drive. In a pivotal letter explaining his loss of political faith to a friend, written in the summer of 1936 weeks after the Great Purge trials had begun, Trilling commented on the need to "completely overhaul" not just his ideas but also his "whole character." If "every revolution must betray itself," it was because "every good thing and every good man has the seeds of degeneration in it or him."

Trilling is not responsible for Freud's popularity; he presupposed it. Scandalized by the vulgar Marxist tract by Reuben Osborn, *Freud and Marx: A Dialectical Study* (1937), which presented psychoanalysis as an adjunct to Stalinism, Trilling became one of the many who over the succeeding decades took Freudianism to sound the death knell of socialism. It helped that Freud had himself been an Anglophile "since boyhood," as Trilling noted.

Trilling's first public comment on Freud and his significance occurred as part of the memorialization of Freud's 1939 death. Asked by *Kenyon Review* to reflect on the significance of psychoanalysis for literature, Trilling argued that Freud had established a parallel route to liberal complexity to rival the creative artistry that had long been the best guide for those guarding against idealism and simplification. Trilling insisted that Thomas Mann had been wrong to imply that Freud intended to legitimize, let alone unleash, passion; psychoanalysis acknowledged its share in order to civilize and domesticate it. "If Freud discovered the darkness for science he never endorses it," he wrote. Both literature and psychoanalysis were sources of a realistic assessment of human limitation that would allow the refounding of liberalism beyond idealism.

As Trilling saw it, far from being a liberator on behalf of love and sex alone, Freud was a stern moralist conceding aggression and death their inevitable shadow over love and life. Freud's later theorizing that posited inborn hatred, so controversial among psychoanalysts, moved beyond the simpleminded idea that realism is about managing pleasure so that its pursuit neither destabilizes civilization nor is so vigilantly policed in its name to lead to neurosis.

For Trilling, this recognition of basic human aggression—"the crown of Freud's broader speculation on the life of man," Trilling wrote—entailed tragic limits to high aspirations in personal and political life, and dictated "the small and controlled administration of pain to inure ourselves to the greater doses which life will force upon us." If love and hate were in permanent standoff, a liberal idealism that failed to incorporate a sense of its own limits suppressed the complexity and variety that literature registered, while also putting civilization itself at risk when it played into the hands of its enemies. "Not being simple, [man] is not simply good," Trilling concluded. "He has, as Freud says somewhere, a kind of hell within him from which rise everlastingly the impulses which threaten his civilization."

TRILLING BEGAN to mobilize Freud to reform liberalism in this way well before World War II, but he repeated these arguments over the next decade and throughout *The Liberal Imagination*, in which the *Kenyon Review* Freud essay was reprinted. Trilling found it especially appalling, therefore, when some tried to rebuild political hope within psychoanalysis, as if Freud's perspective had not wrecked it definitively.

In 1942, for example, Trilling dismissed psychoanalyst Karen Horney's progressivist revisions as "symptomatic" of "one of the great inadequacies of liberal thought, the need for optimism." Prettifying the sink of human evil and pretending that individuals could save themselves from pathology was a reversal of the whole point of psychoanalysis, far beyond the examination room. "Her denial or attenuation of most of Freud's concepts is the response to the wishes of an intellectual class which has always found Freud's ideas cogent but too stringent and too dark," Trilling charged, crediting the founder for "daring to present man with the terrible truth of his own nature," and condemning the follower for doubts.

Freudianism also affected the theory of freedom. Trilling's approach to the concept was different—in some ways opposite—from Berlin's theory of "negative liberty." According to psychoanalysis, Trilling argues, people are constrained in the control they can win from their passions and should have in their self-making, and they must use what freedom they do have for the sake of self-control. "The Freudian man may not be as free as we should like," Trilling surmised, "but at least he has insides." To put a more positive spin on it, Trilling took Freud to be saying that responsible freedom was won in and through bowing to necessity and exercising self-management. As Trilling put it beautifully in a review of Freud's last book on the front page of the *New York Times Book Review* in 1949, "Like any tragic poet, like any true moralist, Freud took it as one of his tasks to define the borders of necessity in order to establish the realm of freedom." Cold War liberalism may call for noninterference from the outside but is premised on interference with oneself.

But Trilling's call for a self-purgation of liberal hope arguably functioned too well—so well, in fact, that anti-utopianism became its own form of tragedy, with a need to submit to "reality" part of the delusion.

One could even speculate, in a psychoanalytic spirit, that Trilling's path to defending a liberalism of constraints and limits, obsessed by the likelihood that good ideals would be perverted into evil outcomes, reflected not so much insight into eternal human nature as Trilling's own ideological trauma. He was an idealist so appalled by the experience of the 1930s that he rationalized out of it a new form of liberalism—like so many others who became what Shklar called "survivalists," prioritizing safety and self-preservation amid the ruins of expectation. The result was a liberalism with few hopes, disturbed by ideological passion, frightened of risk, and indentured to stability—all surrounded by an Arnoldian frame that counseled elites to teach idealists that Western civilization was worth protecting and threatened mainly by their own false optimism.

STILL, TRILLING's critique of his former idealism mourned its loss. He couldn't altogether relinquish the liberalism he struggled to make more "mature" and "realistic"—to use two of his favorite words. Trilling's wartime essay on Tacitus, inspired by the publication of his classicist colleague Moses Hadas's Modern Library edition of the Roman historian's works, provides the best evidence. Tacitus, Trilling observes, was above all a psychologist; he refused to look past death and pain. With the jaundiced eye he cast on imperial folly, Tacitus counseled emotional control, contemplatively rising above it. But Trilling also insisted that the Roman historian consciously understood himself to come *in the aftermath* of an idealism he could preserve only through noting its absence—its unavailability to later, "mature" observers. "The republic had died before his grandfather was born," Trilling wrote, "and he looked back on it as through a haze of idealization" in "an aftermath which had no end." The postwar Marxist Theodor Adorno, himself in mourning, famously remarked that philosophy "lives on because the moment to realize it was missed." One might say that Trilling saw Tacitus making the same rueful observation about contemplation in relation to action: the only thing now was to mourn in the ruins of aspiration.

Arnold had opened *Culture and Anarchy* by calling himself "a liberal tempered by experience, reflection, and renouncement." Trilling presented Cold War liberalism that way, but he also acknowledged the costs of renunciation. From this same perspective, in his celebrated reading of William Wordsworth's "Immortality Ode," Trilling expressed ambivalence about the political choices he was making in his path to Cold War liberalism, preserving idealism only by cutting himself off from it, with "sorrow of giving up an old habit of vision for a new one."

It is perhaps Trilling's 1947 novel *The Middle of the Journey* that provides the best aperture on his ambivalent renunciation of youthful hope. The conventional reading views the novel as an *apologia pro vita sua*, a defense of Trilling's own path. But more plausibly, the novel reveals that Trilling did not believe in simpleminded transcendence of liberal radicalism. His achievement of Cold War liberalism was complex—even self-hating.

Set in the 1930s, the novel traces three trajectories through progressive aspiration. One is an idealistic tenacity that refuses to learn what the communist flirtation teaches about its own false expectations, another a conservative turn that goes to the opposite extreme, and a final one—Trilling's own—that retains a liberal outlook while correcting for earlier enthusiasm.

The book is a thoroughly Freudian affair. Drafted in 1946–7, the project began, Trilling later recalled, as a novella "about death—about what had happened to the way death is conceived by the enlightened consciousness of the modern age." It opens with John Laskell, the reforming liberal, going to Connecticut with his progressive friends to convalesce after a battle with scarlet fever. Trilling explores a death drive that leads humanity to desire death and work toward it. Laskell is fascinated and troubled by his recollection that he had never been happier in life as when he was on the brink of extinction, near the dissolution of self that was paradoxically comparable to the antediluvian joy of "unborn children." In this, it is hard not to hear Trilling dramatizing Freud's theory that the death drive *returns* through a dissolution of life. In view of this drive, Freud was forced to "abandon the belief" in "an impulse towards perfection," because of the tempting "backward path that leads to complete satisfaction"—not merely of the womb, but of what Laskell calls "not being born."

In contrast there are the naive progressives, who stand for life in a pure and unalloyed sense—always looking forward, not in an aftermath without end but a prologue to an unending future. When Laskell arrives in Connecticut, his progressive caretakers cannot even bring themselves to use the word "death," a horror beyond contemplating. "Life could have no better representatives" than these liberals, the narrator says, and they certainly are represented as confused—in denial about the limits antagonism and mortality impose. Their "passionate expectation of the future," in the name of those "all over the world, suffering, or soon to suffer," is morally obtuse. Reforming liberalism is repeatedly likened to accepting the reality of death, for example when Laskell struggles to explain to his caretakers what it meant for their conservative friend to abandon utopianism: "People actually do die." The novel is also, of course, about avoiding becoming "the blackest of reactionaries" in the process—like the real-life conservative model of Cold War convert Whittaker Chambers—but even that is represented as being more open to death and experience than unreformed liberalism. "You couldn't live the life of promises without yourself remaining a child," Laskell learns.

For all its insistence that liberals accept mature wisdom, the novel never puts to rest the possibility that the child is the father of the man. Laskell's own self-reform, as he adjusts his optimism about helping others to fit with what he learns from reflecting on death, is anything but triumphant; it is merely better than the alternatives of progressive optimism and Christian pessimism, since neither childish innocence about the human condition nor adult acceptance of death seem plausible. Moreover, the novel dramatizes Trilling's disappointment with his own limiting decision to become a literary critic. He takes an exceptional foray into literature—*The Middle of the Journey* is the only literary text he would write—to portray a protagonist who abandons a youthful desire for literary achievement for the mature role of technocrat, never being "great" and only "useful." "When I do write, I'm just a critic of other people's work," Laskell remarks at one point. "Critics make life miserable for people," a child replies.

Perhaps most revealing, the novel ends by *mourning* the death of idealism, which is very different than just giving it up as a mistake. The child who makes a dig at critics, it turns out, has a heart ailment she doesn't know about. At the climax of the novel, she dies. The progressive caretakers cannot recognize the event as tragic because they cannot accept death—or the guilt of those who are complicit with it—even when they witness it. The convert to Christianity sees the child's hope as a false lure, for all people are sinners. Laskell's truth is about remaining dispassionate and uncommitted, but it is also about living through the death of idealism and, while marking its limits, mourning its loss ever after. Cold War liberalism's entanglement from an idealism it could never disavow entirely made it a bereaved liberalism.

In her memoir of their life together, Diana Trilling wondered whether her husband's "friends and colleagues had no hint of how deeply he scorned the very qualities of character—his quiet, his moderation, his gentle reasonableness—for which he was most admired in his lifetime and which have been most celebrated since his death." They might have gotten some hint had they read his novel.

TRILLING RETURNED to Freud again and again through the Cold War, evolving his "uses" for psychoanalysis as his own stance was buffeted by challenging events and generational change. In 1953, in spite of all his hard work, Trilling complained that "Freud's doctrine has been with us for nearly fifty years and it contains the elements for a most complex moral system, yet I know of no attempt to deal seriously with its implications, especially its moral implications." That call was taken up most directly by Philip Rieff (at the time, Susan Sontag's husband), whose *Freud: The Mind of the Moralist* (1959) defined its era. Rieff's publisher pulled enthusiastic lines of Trilling's reader's report as a cover endorsement. For Rieff, who referred to Trilling as collective "teacher," Freud was a moral educator, ushering in the age of "psychological man" and a disconsolate happiness within the terms of hopelessness.

Attempts to marry Marx and Freud became popular in the 1960s. Though he was dismissed as a "lightweight" in intellectual historian Paul Robinson's 1969 survey of such ventures, *The Freudian Left*, Trilling nonetheless took detailed notes on the book, focusing on the criticism of *Civilization and Its Discontents* offered by Herbert Marcuse and Wilhelm Reich it summarized. The effort helped Trilling prepare for the defense of his version of psychoanalysis in his last and most significant book, *Sincerity and Authenticity*, published in 1972 three years before his death. Tracing ideals of self-knowledge and self-realization, Trilling warned against the increasing popularity of making Freud serve progressive causes. The entire point of psychoanalysis, Trilling insisted, was to impose the limits of harsh self-discipline on expectations of change.

Over the decades Trilling's readers have wondered whether, by establishing a Cold War liberalism only a hair's breadth from conservatism and indeed neoconservatism, he prepared their ascendancy. Literary critic Joseph Frank, for one, conceded that Trilling had achieved perfect equipoise between left and right in *The Liberal Imagination*, but he also argued that Trilling quickly moved from a vision of literature educating politics to one in which culture displaced politics. If Trilling had once made room for constraint in the name of credible liberty, soon "for man's own protection Mr. Trilling keeps recalling him to his earth-bound condition." Freud's aura had enabled Trilling to do so "without feeling it as a self-betrayal."

And as a matter of fact, Trilling's work did have direct relations to the origins of neoconservatism (which had its true roots in the 1930s and 1940s rather than merely in response to the 1960s), even if Trilling himself never went all the way. Irving Kristol published one of his earliest essays on Trilling in 1944, reserving highest praise for Trilling's denunciation of a self-righteous liberalism that reached "a kind of disgust with humanity as it is" in the name of "a perfect faith in humanity as it is to be." Kristol's partner Gertrude Himmelfarb, who expended all her energies to conscript Trilling retroactively into the neoconservative movement and then cast herself as his devoted follower, testified how deeply she had been shaped by the edgy piece that Kristol discussed.

Far more important than the extent of Trilling's links to conservatism or neoconservatism, however, is the way he fundamentally refashioned liberalism itself, the political and psychological goal closest to his heart. In this he epitomized all Cold War liberals, who *themselves* insisted that the liberalism they had inherited required drastic renovation and revision: a break from the liberal past in the name of liberal survival. By renouncing what had once made liberalism radical in a twin move of resignation and self-protection, Trilling cut himself off from the hopes he had once nurtured, even as he memorialized them.

Is that all we can do? Liberalism's nineteenth- and early twentieth-century strains—the ones that Trilling self-consciously overthrew—are better places to start in exploring liberalism's far reaches. Emancipatory before the Cold War—a doctrine committed most of all to free and equal self-creation, as well as accepting of democracy and welfare (though never enough to date)—liberalism can be something other, something far more, than the Cold War liberalism it has become.

The founders of liberalism in the nineteenth century—such as Benjamin Constant, John Stuart Mill, and Alexis de Tocqueville—had been Romantics committed above all to a culture of individuality and self-making among free and equal citizens. Like Trilling, the personal was political for them, and they sought political institutions that were supposed to make the self-making they cared most about more likely. Very much unlike other Cold War liberals, who often blamed Romanticism for totalitarianism, Trilling responded to his ideological trauma by refusing to abandon it. Instead, he buried this earlier liberalism deep in his psyche, setting up controls that would keep it from the devastation he thought psychic aggression would lead to. But why live in sorrow for what we have to give up, especially if it is not as risky as Trilling supposed?

Whether liberalism deserves to survive depends entirely on whether it can recover what Trilling preserved from the controls he mistakenly placed on it. If liberalism is to be freed from its Cold War foreshortening, one advocate for doing so might be Trilling himself.

BEHIND THE IRON WALL
A. Dirk Moses

IN THE WAKE of Hamas's October 7 attack in Israel, an international genocide debate has been unleashed. Some in the field of genocide studies, including Israeli historian Raz Segal and British sociologist Martin Shaw, have argued that Israel's retaliatory assault on Gaza constitutes genocide. Palestinian and international legal academics, and increasing numbers of commentators (including Jewish voices), also claim that genocide is imminent or already underway, and the Center for Constitutional Rights is suing the U.S. government for failing to prevent genocide in Gaza. Before and after them, other international legal experts issued a statement condemning Hamas's massacre of 1,200 Israelis as itself genocidal, and a group of scholars of the Holocaust wrote that the acts brought to mind "the pogroms that paved the way to the Final Solution."

The point of genocide claims is not only legal and strategic but—as with the Russian invasion of Ukraine and the Chinese treatment of Uyghur citizens—urgent and moral, concerned both with saving lives or stemming humanitarian disaster. As I write, Gaza is being destroyed by Israeli bombs and missiles, Palestinian civilian casualties are mounting by the hour—over 11,000, more than two-thirds women and children—hospitals have been targeted, and humanitarian workers and journalists are being killed. Over a million Palestinians have been displaced, and Israeli armed forces are invading. Meanwhile Israeli settlers and authorities have unleashed a wave of terror on West Bank Palestinians. "The day of revenge is coming," declare masked men as they murder and expel Palestinians from their villages.

In addition to debates among legal experts, a global protest movement—the largest since the Second Gulf War—has emerged, decrying Israel's actions as genocidal and demanding a ceasefire. This genocide claim expresses outrage and grief about the destruction of bare, less "grievable" life, seeks to generate political pressure to rein in Israeli ambitions, and hopes eventually to generate international legal accountability. It also seeks to incriminate Israeli military violence by placing it in the same frame as the Holocaust, the paradigm case of genocide. For that reason, a Palestinian academic in Gaza, Haidar Eid, wrote on October 10 that the conflict is "our Warsaw Uprising moment." In response, Israeli commentators reversed the equation by comparing their country's bombing of Gaza to the British destruction of Dresden during World War II. For them, Palestinians, not Israelis, are the Nazis in this fatal drama.

Yet the legal question helps to explain why this claim of genocide has not gained significant traction beyond the protest movement. International law sets a high standard for proving genocide charges, suggesting this "crime of crimes" is a rare act of "rogue" states. In reality, acts of collective punishment, deportation, and even destruction of peoples lie at the foundation of modern states. Some of the many cases that abound through history meet today's definition of genocide, but most do not. In this respect, the genocide frame on the violence that has erupted both on and since October 7 is fundamentally limited by the concept's legal parameters. Anyone concerned with civilian protection must consider the broader history of state violence and violent resistance, and their connections to Israel and Gaza today.

MASS STATE VIOLENCE against civilians is not a glitch in the international system; it is baked into statehood itself. The natural right of self-defense plays a foundational role in the self-conception of Western states in particular, the formation of which is inseparable from imperial expansion. Since the Spanish conquest of the Americas starting in the sixteenth century, settlers justified their reprisals against indigenous resistance as defensive "self-preservation." If they felt their survival was imperiled, colonizers engaged in massive retaliation against native peoples, including noncombatants. The doctrine of double effect assured them that killing innocents was permissible as a side effect of carrying out a moral end, like self-defense.

They understood their presence in far-off lands as legitimate, based on civilizational and racial hierarchies. Native resistance was framed as illegitimate and terroristic. The Spanish thought they had been mandated by God to spread the faith and were thus justified in annexing all territories not populated by Christians in order to convert the heathens. As they saw it, the natives in the jungle, not the settlers, were the aggressors. By the nineteenth century, the Christianizing mission had been augmented by a civilizing one of the "savage" natives. More recently, this colonial ideology has manifested itself in the project of "bringing democracy to the Arab world," with Israel designated as the "the only democracy in the Middle East," the proverbial "villa in the jungle."

The colonial wars that won Europe most of the globe by the early 1900s enabled the breakthrough of the European modern state. Without imperial possessions and the lucrative trade in sugar and other commodities predicated on the Atlantic slave trade, European states would not have generated the surpluses necessary to pay for their military establishments and the bureaucratic apparatuses required to sustain them. And while European powers and settlers in their colonies did not set out to exterminate the peoples they conquered, they killed any who resisted, claiming that their hands were forced.

A number of lessons can be drawn from this history of expansion and mass violence. The first is that civilian destruction tends to be greatest when security retaliation reaches the level of what I have called "permanent security"—extreme responses by states to security threats, enacted in the name of self-defense. Permanent security actions target entire civilian populations under the logic of ensuring that terrorists and insurgents can never again represent a threat. It is a project, in other words, that seeks to avert future threats by anticipating them today. Such aspirations are evident in many ongoing humanitarian crises. Vladimir Putin reasons that Ukraine must be forcibly returned to the Russian orbit so it cannot serve as a launching site for NATO missiles decades from now. The Myanmarese military sought to squash separatism once and for all by expelling the Rohingya minority in 2017. And the leaders of the Communist Party of China seek to "pacify" and "reeducate" Uyghurs by mass incarceration to forestall independence strivings forever.

The second lesson is that particularly vicious reprisals occur when indigenous resistance involves attacks on the colonizer's families—on women and children. The campaigns waged against the "Indian Mutiny" of 1857–1859, the Boxer Rebellion in China of 1900, and the Herero uprising in German Southwest Africa from 1904 to 1907 all evidence this. Adding to the bloodshed is the fact that this kind of unyielding, zero-sum demographic struggle is often exactly what is prescribed by the violent millenarian resistance movements that arise in the wake of social breakdown prompted by colonial rule. Such movements tend to view the colonizers as a single hostile entity, making settler families as targetable as military and police personnel. What some historians call "subaltern genocide," genocide against the colonizers, has arisen in precisely these conditions of asymmetric power and violence.

As an analytical matter, it is clear that resistance is the consequence of enduring occupation or colonial rule. Observing as much does not at all justify attacks on civilians as a normative or legal matter. The historical record shows that, however terrible, violent anticolonial uprisings were invariably smashed with far greater violence than they unleashed. The violence of the "civilized" is far more effective than the violence of the "barbarians" and "savages." The suppression of the Maji Maji uprising in German East Africa between 1905 and 1907, for example, caused at least 75,000 and perhaps 300,000 African fatalities. Throughout the five-hundred-year history of Western empires, the security of European colonizers has trumped the security and independence of the colonized.

WHAT DOES all this mean in the case of Israel and Gaza today?

Many Hamas officials seem to have taken a millenarian position on violent resistance, even if the organization is now prepared to negotiate about hostages. In an interview on Arab television, former Hamas politburo chairman Khaled Mashal suggested that anticolonial struggles can last over a century and cost millions of lives. Admitting that Hamas had not consulted Palestinian Gazans about the October 7 attack, he insinuated that they must nonetheless pay the price of national liberation: "no nation is liberated without sacrifices." When asked about the massacre of Israeli civilians, he replied that civilian casualties occur in war and that Hamas is "not responsible for them," refusing to acknowledge the atrocities committed by Hamas forces.

As for Israel, its security analysts have long pursued a strategy of attrition to contain Palestinian resistance, a strategy they referred to as "mowing the grass"—targeted assassination and occasional bombing. The outlook is the contemporary expression of Vladimir

Jabotinsky's famous "Iron Wall" argument from 1923, in which the Revisionist Zionist leader argued that Palestinian resistance was understandable, inevitable—and anticolonial. Speaking of Palestinians, Jabotinsky wrote that "they feel at least the same instinctive jealous love of Palestine, as the old Aztecs felt for ancient Mexico, and their Sioux for their rolling Prairies." Because Palestinians could not be bought off with material promises, Jabotinsky wanted the British Mandate authorities to enable Zionist colonization until Jews, then a tiny minority of Palestine, reached a majority. "Zionist colonisation must either stop, or else proceed regardless of the native population," he concluded. "Which means that it can proceed and develop only under the protection of a power that is independent of the native population—behind an iron wall, which the native population cannot breach."

Hamas breached the "iron wall" of the Gaza border on October 7. In response, we are now witnessing the crystallization of Israel's attempt at a permanent security solution. Having failed to "manage the conflict," and interpreting Hamas's massacre as a Holocaust-like trauma, its leaders are now declaring that these Palestinian "Nazis" should never again pose a threat to Israel. With its air and ground assaults, the Israeli government seeks not only to destroy Hamas as a political and military entity—a security aim—but to corral much, if not the entire, Palestinian population to southern Gaza possibly in order to make a permanent buffer zone of the north and, eventually, to push Gazans across the border into Egypt.

The strategic logic is presumably that the pressure of the ensuing humanitarian disaster will force the UN and especially the Arab world to resettle Palestinians—a permanent security aim. A think tank close to the government, the Misgav Institute for National Security and Zionist Strategy, has already formulated a grand plan to this end. A far-right Israeli minister even advocates recolonizing Gaza with Jewish settlers. In other words, to ensure that Palestinian militants can never again attack Israel, its armed forces are subjecting two million Palestinians to serial war crimes and mass expulsion. "Our goal is victory," Israeli prime minister Benjamin Netanyahu declared on October 16, "a crushing victory over Hamas, toppling its regime and removing its threat to the State of Israel once and for all." The Minister of Defense, Benny Gantz, echoed this notion: "Israel cannot accept such an active threat on its borders." Already on October 14, the United Nations Special Rapporteur on the situation of human rights in the occupied Palestinian Territories warned of a new Nakba. Israeli leaders have embraced this language themselves. Avi Dichter, agricultural minister and a member of the security cabinet, spoke this week of "rolling out the Gaza Nakba." Before him, Knesset member Ariel Kallner wrote on social media, "Right now, one goal: Nakba! A Nakba that will overshadow the Nakba of 48. Nakba in Gaza and Nakba to anyone who dares to join!"

If Western states support this solution for Israeli permanent security—as the United States appears to be with its budgeting of refugee support in neighboring countries under the guise of a "humanitarian" gesture—they will be continuing a venerable tradition. During, between, and after both twentieth-century world wars, large-scale population transfers and exchanges took place across the Eurasian continent to radically homogenize empires and nations.

Millions of people fled or were expelled or transferred from Turkey, Greece, Austria, Italy, India, Palestine, Central and Eastern Europe. Progressive Europeans reasoned then that long-term peace would be secured if troublesome minorities were removed. This ideology—which the governments of Russia, China, Turkey, India, and Sri Lanka share today—maintains that indigenous and minority populations must submit to their subordination and, if they resist, face subjugation, deportation, or destruction. Antiterrorism operations that kill thousands of civilians are taken to be acceptable responses to terrorist operations that kill far fewer civilians.

Indigenous and occupied peoples, then, are placed in an impossible position. If they resist with violence, they are violently put down. If they do not, states will overlook the lower-intensity but unrelenting violence to which they are subject. Right now, Western and even many Arab states are prepared to indefinitely tolerate the unbearable conditions in Gaza and the West Bank while attempting to broker a lasting peace in the Middle East without resolving the Palestinian struggle for liberation, whatever form that might take. "There is violence in this insistence on nonviolence by the international community," Abdaljawad Omar, a graduate student at Birzeit University in Ramallah, wrote on November 9, "because it is effectively an invitation for Palestinians to lie down and die."

Indeed, nonviolent resistance to this state of affairs is ignored, demonized, and brutally suppressed. Many U.S. states and Germany virtually criminalize the Boycott, Divestment and Sanctions movement as anti-Semitic, for example. The March of Return in Gaza from 2018 to 2019 was met with Israeli sniper fire that killed 233 and injured and maimed nearly 6,000 Palestinians. Local Palestinian leaders who advocate nonviolent protection of their communities from settlers, like Issa Amro in Hebron, are harassed by Israeli authorities. As Middle East analyst Helena Cobban has observed in these pages, Hamas thus reasons that Palestinians have nothing to gain by conforming to a U.S.-led "rules-based international order" that has forgotten about them.

THE TOTALITY of these considerations suggests some of the limitations of the ongoing genocide debate. While the concept of genocide is used by scholars in a broader explanatory sense, it is also being invoked today as a legal category to accuse Israel of the gravest international crime. While actions can be condemned as genocidal for political mobilization, legally speaking a genocide cannot be unilaterally declared. Rather, courts prosecute individuals for acts of genocide, usually along with war crimes and crimes against humanity. That time may well come. Karim Khan, the International Criminal Court's prosecutor, has declared that the court has jurisdiction over the territory on which the conflict is taking place and that he is observing the conflict closely. But so far, he is talking generally about war crimes, not genocide.

Should Khan go looking for evidence to support the claim of genocide that has been advanced against Israel, it might seem that he does not need to look very far. Israeli politicians and military personnel have made numerous statements with genocidal connotations, asserting the depravity ("human animals") and collective guilt of Palestinians in Gaza for Hamas's mass murder of Israelis on October 7. On October 28 Netanyahu compared Hamas to Israel's Biblical enemy Amalek. "Now go and smite Amalek," reads the Biblical passage, "and utterly destroy all that they have, and spare them not; but slay both man and woman, infant and suckling, ox and sheep, camel and ass." It is sometimes forgotten that the United Nations Convention on the Punishment and Prevention of the Crime of Genocide (UNGC) of 1948 prohibits "direct and public incitement to commit genocide." A former IDF intelligence officer observed that "just as Hamas removed all red lines in targeting civilians, so too will Israel retaliate."

Even so, proving that individual Israelis have committed acts of genocide is extraordinarily difficult given the parameters set by international law. That is no accident. When state parties to the UNGC negotiated in 1947 and 1948, they distinguished genocidal intent from military necessity, so that states could wage the kind of wars that Russia and Israel are conducting today and avoid prosecution for genocide. The high legal standard stems from the restrictive UNGC definition of genocide, which was modeled on the Holocaust and requires that a perpetrator intend to "destroy, in whole or in part, a national, ethnical, racial or religious group, as such" (the *dolus specialis*) in at least one of five prescribed ways (the *actus reus*). The words "as such" are widely regarded as imposing a stringent intent requirement: an act counts as genocide only if individuals are targeted solely by virtue of their group membership—like Jews during World War II—and not for strategic reasons like suppressing an insurgency. Despite many assertions of Palestinian collective guilt by Israeli leaders, they also insist that the IDF targets Hamas as a security threat, and not Palestinians "as such." If the Holocaust is unique, as commonly asserted, how are other cases of mass violence against civilians supposed to measure up? The point is that it is very difficult to do so.

In other words, states would not permit the UNGC to inhibit their right to pursue permanent security, whether against internal or external enemies. The staggering scale of postwar violence perpetrated with impunity testifies to their success. It is true that states agreed on other instruments, like the Geneva Conventions, as a "restraint in war," but they have also done their best to avoid such restraints. Together, the United States and Russia have killed many millions of civilians in their respective imperial wars in Korea, Vietnam, and Chechnya; so have postcolonial states like Nigeria and Pakistan in fighting secessions. Genocide allegations were leveled in some of these cases in global campaigns like the one we see now, but none stuck, and they are largely forgotten in the annals of mass violence against civilians. That prospect faces Palestine advocates today, because successful analogies with the Holocaust are virtually impossible to make—especially by Palestinians against Israel, for which the Holocaust memory is a state project.

Adding to the difficulty of establishing genocidal intent is the uncertainty in international humanitarian law about the legality of civilians killed "incidentally" in the course of attacking legitimate military targets. While the majority of international lawyers agree that civilian deaths are acceptable so long as they are not disproportionate in relation to the military advantage sought, others argue that bombing crowded marketplaces and hospitals regardless of military objective is necessarily indiscriminate and thus illegal.

Needless to say, Israeli officials insist that they abide by international law by targeting only Hamas and issuing warnings to civilians. Their order for Palestinians to move to the south of Gaza has also been defended as an attempt to separate the civilian population from Hamas fighters. Most Western states—including the United States—accept this reasoning, finding that Hamas's use of "human shields" to be the relevant cause of civilian casualties and thereby justifying Israel's indiscriminate attacks. They go far in excusing all Israeli conduct in the name of its legitimate self-defense; the US even seems to have demurred on whether the Geneva Conventions are applicable to Palestinian territories. It is thus unsurprising that they have not pressed the Israeli government to explain how cutting off water, food, and power to Gaza—a "war of starvation" as the Euro-Med Human Rights Monitor put it—is a legitimate military tactic, one not covered by the UNGC, which declares one genocidal predicate act to be "deliberately inflicting on the group conditions of life calculated to bring about its physical destruction in whole or in part." But if so-called humanitarian pauses are occurring to allow in a little, if grossly inadequate, aid, and the "total siege" is lifted after the military defeat of Hamas (should it happen), it will be difficult to argue in a legal context that Israel's strangling of Gaza was a genocidal act.

The Israeli human rights group Breaking the Silence has observed the operation less of genocide than of a particularly brutal form of deterrence: the "Dahiya Doctrine," which, they argue, dictates "disproportionate attacks, including against civilian structures and infrastructure." This is clearly illegal. Making a similar point, American journalist Thomas Friedman wrote in an op-ed that Israel's conduct was designed to signal to its enemies that none could "outcrazy" it. To specify what he meant, he coined the term "Hama rules," referring to Syrian president Hafez al-Assad's ruthless killing of 20,000 Islamist rebels in the town of Hama in 1982. On this counting, Israel is well on the way to reaching that terrible total. Excessive reprisals, we should recall, are a staple of colonial warfare and state consolidation.

Regardless of any legal question of genocide, Israel's supporters find themselves tacitly condoning the ongoing slaughter of thousands of Palestinian civilians. A considerable portion of their publics understandably reject this outrageous state of affairs. They are unimpressed by legal hairsplitting about the UNGC's requirement that people are killed "as such," meaning solely on the grounds of their identity—the genocidal intent of destroying the enemy—rather than by the military logic of defeating them. For the fact is that whether Israel is committing genocide or erecting a new "iron wall" of defense, masses of Palestinians are being killed and possibly expelled. It is a distinction without a difference for the victims.

Seen in this light, the protest movement's allegation of genocide can be understood as a symptom of the "utter failure of international law in responding to war crimes and crimes against humanity (including apartheid)," as legal scholar Itamar Mann has observed. The claim also reflects the "truth" of the victim's perspective. Since genocide is a synonym for the destruction of peoples, whether the killing and suppression of their culture is motivated by destruction "as such" or by deterrence, the experience is the same: a destructive attack on a people, and not just random civilians. But the UNGC does not reflect the victim's perspective. It protects the perpetrators: states that seek permanent security.

SO FAR, most Western states have done the same, closing ranks in support of Israel. Hamas is solely responsible for the current conflict, they say. Missing from this view has been a recognition of any of the history that led to it. For instance, most Palestinians in Gaza are not Gazans but refugees from the Zionist cleansing of their villages in 1948. Those who want to go back to them, now destroyed, recall the UN General Assembly Resolution 194 (III) of December 11, 1948, which reads that Palestinian "refugees wishing to return to their homes and live at peace with their neighbours should be permitted to do so at the earliest practicable date." Neither have most states in the Global South have forgotten the Palestinian right of self-determination. They ask not only whether Israel has a right to exist—which is the usual question in the West—but whether Palestine does as well. For this reason, while they deplore Hamas's murder of Israeli civilians, they do not regard the attack as "unprovoked," like most Western states. Of course, Hamas's atrocious attacks make the prospect of living peaceably with Israeli neighbors impossible for the moment.

The Jewish historian of nationalism Hans Kohn observed a similar state of affairs when he left Palestine after the 1929 massacre of Jews in Hebron. Like Jabotinsky, he understood the violence as a colonial uprising. Unlike Jabotinsky, he thought Zionist colonization behind the iron wall of the British military was untenable, because it was erected against the majority Arab population and would provoke endless colonial warfare. The terrible events since October 7—and indeed since the Zionist project of demographically restructuring Mandate Palestine via mass immigration beginning in the 1920s—testify to his prescience.

Kohn's vision of a binational state in Palestine was dashed by the "iron wall" logic of other Zionists. Today the Palestinian political theorist Bashir Bashir talks of "egalitarian binationalism" as a workable arrangement that respects the independent nationalities of Palestinians and Israelis while binding them in an equitable polity. Maybe the ghost of Kohn could return one day. In the meantime, we must recognize that the law of genocide does not exhaust the morally abhorrent operations of permanent security. Unless the conditions of permanent insecurity are confronted, permanent security aspirations and practices will haunt Palestinians and Israelis.

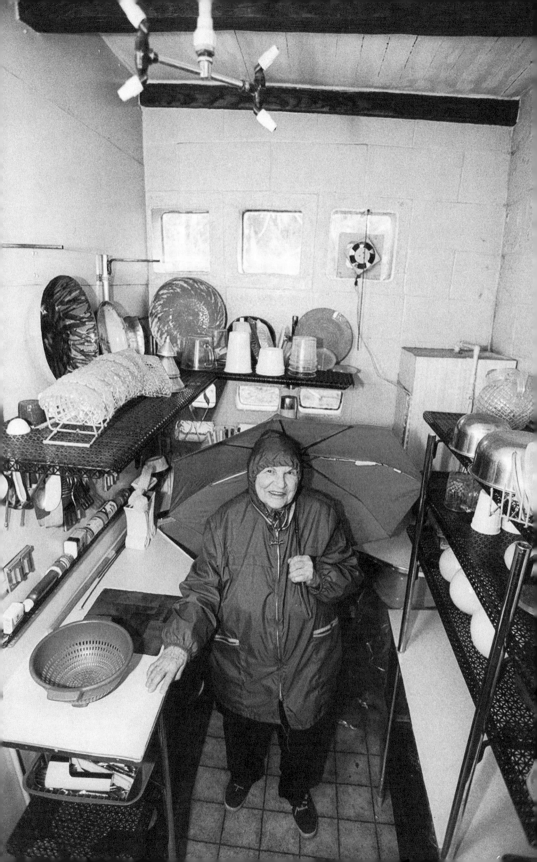

A WORLD WITHOUT WORK
Rachel Fraser

IN 1980 Frances Gabe applied for a patent for a self-cleaning house. The design was based on her own home, which she had worked on for more than a decade. Each room had a sprinkler system installed; at the push of a button, Gabe could send sudsy water pouring over her specially treated furniture. Clean water would then wash the soap away, before draining from the gently sloped floors. Blasts of warm air would dry the room in less than an hour, and the used water flowed into the kennel, to give the Great Dane a bath.

The problem with most houses, Gabe thought, was that they were designed by men, who would never be tasked with cleaning them. The self-cleaning house, she hoped, would free women from the "nerve-twangling bore" of housework. Such hopes are widely shared: a 2019 survey found that self-cleaning homes were the most eagerly anticipated of all speculative technologies.

Cleaning, like cooking, childbearing, and breastfeeding, is a paradigm case of reproductive labor. Reproductive labor is a special form of work. It doesn't itself produce commodities (coffee pots, silicon chips); rather, it's the form of work that creates and maintains labor power itself, and hence makes the production of commodities possible in the first place. Reproductive labor is low-prestige and (typically) either poorly paid or entirely unwaged. It's also obstinately feminized: both within the social imaginary and in actual fact, most reproductive labor is done by women. It is perhaps unsurprising, then, that political discussions of work often treat reproductive labor as an afterthought.

One place this elision shows up is in the "post-work" tradition. For the post-work tradition—whose influence on the Anglo-American left has been growing for the last decade—the aim of radical politics should not (just) be for higher wages, more secure employment, or more generous parental leave. Rather, radical politics should aim for a world in which work's social role is utterly transformed and highly attenuated—a world in which work can no longer serve as either a disciplining institution or as the fulcrum for our social identities.

Two new publications bookend the tradition. Paul Lafargue's 1880 essay, "The Right to Be Lazy"—a touchstone for post-work theorists—was recently reprinted in a new translation by Alex Andriesse. (A Cuban-born revolutionary socialist, Lafargue married one of Karl Marx's daughters, Laura, in 1868.) Helen Hester and Nick Srnicek offer a more contemporary contribution. In *After Work: A History of the Home and the Fight for Free Time*, they blend post-work conviction with feminist scruples. A post-work politics must, they argue, have something to say about reproductive labor. The post-work tradition grapples with the grandest themes in politics—the interplay between freedom and necessity. But within its lofty imaginaries, there must also be space for a dishcloth, and a changing table.

AUTOMATION HAS always been central to the post-work imaginary. In "The Soul of Man Under Socialism" (1891), Oscar Wilde envisages a world in which "the machine" is made to "work for us in coal mines, and do all sanitary services, and be the stoker of steamers, and clean the streets, and run messages on wet days, and do anything that is tedious or distressing." But Wilde gives little thought to the soul of *woman* under socialism. While the machine frees men from "that sordid necessity of living for others," it does not lend a hand with the laundry, or feeding the baby. Even in the age of the machine, it seems, women are mopping up after others.

Maybe Wilde thought breastfeeding would be harder to automate than coalmining. But even if we could automate reproductive labor, it's not clear that we *should*. It's one thing to imagine robots taking over the factory, the warehouse, and the office. But, as Hester and Srnicek point out, it's quite another to envisage them in charge of the hospital, the nursing home, or the kindergarten. A world where no one spends tedious hours on the assembly line is a world worth aspiring to. But a world where no one nurses their children or cooks food for their friends? That sounds like a nightmare.

Reproductive labor, then, resists automation. Can we still aspire to a world without work? One might argue that reproductive labor is not really work (because it is unwaged, or because it happens inside the home, or because it is bound up with love) and therefore lies beyond the scope of a post-work politics. Hester and Srnicek are (rightly) unconvinced. Reproductive labor is work—and work that we can't offload to a machine. But, they argue, when properly understood, the post-work project can absorb the stubborn realities of reproductive labor; indeed, they write, it "has significant contributions to make to our understanding of how we might better organize the labour of reproduction."

Critiques of capitalism tend to come in one of three flavors. Distributive critiques locate the badness of capitalism in its tendency toward an unjust distribution of goods. Others identify the wrong of exploitation as capitalism's core moral flaw. Hester and Srnicek work within a third critical paradigm, whose key moral grammar is that of *alienation*. Under this rubric, the true badness of work under capitalism—traditional wage labor and unpaid reproductive labor alike—lies in its distortion of our practical natures. When we fashion the world in accordance with our freely chosen ends, we realize ourselves within it. We exercise a key human capacity: the capacity to make ourselves objective. But under capitalism, we are not free to choose and pursue our own ends; we are forced into projects that we value only instrumentally. We mop floors, deliver packages, or babysit not because we think these activities have value in and of themselves, but because we need the money. We act on the world, yes, but we cannot properly *express* ourselves within it.

Hester and Srnicek don't actually talk in terms of alienation. Their critical registers are those of "temporal sovereignty" and "free time." But these are novel placeholders, used to freshly mint an argument for which alienation has been the customary coin. "The struggle against work," they say, "is the fight for free time." And free time matters because, they argue, it is only when we have free time that we can engage in activities that are chosen for their own sake: activities in which we can "recognize ourselves in what we do."

Such activities needn't be leisurely. Someone who composes a sonata might be composing just for the sake of it—laboring with "the most damned seriousness, the most intense exertion." (Here Hester and Srnicek quote the Marx of the *Grundrisse*.) Even dull, menial, and repetitive activities may enter into this "realm of freedom" when they are a constitutive part of appropriately valued projects. "Laboring over a hot stove," Hester and Srnicek write, "can take on the quality of being a freely chosen activity in the arc of a larger self-directed goal." Hester and Srnicek, then, are not advocating indolence. For them, the problem with work is not that it is effortful. Humans are agents. We make and we do. Work, though, catches our making and doing in a trap: it is *caged* agency. Hester and Srnicek want us to open the cage.

HESTER AND SRNICEK's friendliness to effort marks one point of difference between their approach and Lafargue's. For Lafargue, freedom is more closely tied to idleness. Hot stoves don't feature in his post-work world. His vision of the good life centers on lazing about, smoking cigarettes, and feasting.

The differences don't stop there. Hester and Srnicek offer a *moral* critique of capitalism, one that appeals to values. Despite

Lafargue's title, with its talk of a "right," his main focus is political economy. He is best read as offering a "crisis theory" of capitalism: a form of critique that appeals not to moral damage but rather to capitalism's structural instability. Capitalism, says the crisis theorist, is a flawed economic system not because it is (say) cruel, but because it is a self-undermining system. It destroys its own capacity to function.

The roots of crisis, for Lafargue, lie in the inevitable mismatch between the productive capacities of a capitalist society and that society's capacity to consume what is produced. Capitalism, he thinks, requires that workers play two roles: they need to make things, but they also need to buy them. Eventually, these two roles will come into conflict. Suppose that a commodity is overproduced, so that its supply outstrips demand. Its price will fall. To compensate, factory owners will cut costs or slow production. And that means they will pay their workers less or lay them off. Consumer demand will then further contract, incentivizing further wage cuts, which will further suppress demand. Worker and capitalist will both be trapped in an ever-tightening fist of economic dysfunction.

Lafargue's innovation was not to link overproduction with crisis—hardly an original suggestion—but rather lay in his proposed solution. Where twentieth-century Keynesian reformists proposed to coordinate production and consumption by stimulating demand, Lafargue pushes in the opposite direction. We should coordinate by suppressing production; workers should simply work less. Thus, Lafargue posits not so much a *right* to be lazy as a *duty*. Those who shirk it are to blame for overproduction. "The proletarians," he writes, "have given themselves over body and soul to the vices of work [and so] they precipitate the whole of society into those industrial crises of overproduction that convulse the social organism." (This haughty tone is of a piece with the rest of the essay, which is consistently disdainful.)

This argument makes for an unusual brand of crisis theory. Most crisis theorists trace overproduction to *structural* features of the capitalist economy. This underpins their contention that overproduction is not just bad luck but a *sine qua non* of capitalism. "It is in the nature of capital," Marx wrote in *Theories of Surplus Value* (1863), to "drive production to the limit set by the productive forces . . . without any consideration for the actual limits of the market." Insofar as overproduction is sufficient for crisis, then, it will also be "in the nature of capital" to undermine its own productive capacity. For Lafargue, by contrast, overproduction is not a structural necessity but a function of working-class myopia.

Lafargue doesn't worry that suppressing production will lead to scarcity. If the proletariat do manage to withhold their labor, he thinks, then laziness will become not a duty but a default. If workers work less, industrial equipment will be developed more quickly to compensate; and this trend will eventually result in a post-scarcity, post-work idyll. And Lafargue is at best impressionistic as to what life in such a world might be like. The niceties of (say) institutional design are quite beyond his ken. This marks a third point of contrast between Lafargue's essay and *After Work*. Lafargue is primarily focused on the pathologies of industrial capitalism and on how they might be overcome. *After Work*, by contrast, is more interested in providing a blueprint than a roadmap—less concerned with how we might arrive in a post-work world, that is, than with how to organize things once we get there.

AFTER WORK begins with a puzzle. Post-work theorists propose "free time for all!" But what if the parents' free time can only be purchased at the cost of their baby going hungry or unwashed? How can free time for all be secured alongside care for all?

In their attempt to realize both, Hester and Srnicek make three key moves. First, they argue that a lot of reproductive labor is unnecessary. They give the example of ironing. If style norms became more crumple-tolerant, ironing one's shirts could become an optional eccentricity rather than a burdensome chore. And if caring for someone doesn't mean doing their ironing, care and free time become more compatible as goals.

Of course, some reproductive labor is non-negotiable; Hester and Srnicek know this. So they make a second move. Reproductive labor's resistance to automation, they contend, has been overstated by the squeamish (and the privileged). Waged care workers often "point to elements of their jobs that could usefully be automated," giving them more time to focus on the bits of their job that require a genuine human connection. Hester and Srnicek cite surveys showing that pensioners are significantly more open to the use of robots in elder care than other groups are. This is perhaps not surprising when we remember—Hester and Srnicek are careful to remind us—that we should not sentimentalize caring relationships. Many older adults are abused by their caregivers.

Hester and Srnicek are not crude techno-optimists. They realize that tech can be labor-extractive, as well as labor-saving. Despite the "industrial revolution in the home" in the first half of the twentieth century, full-time housewives spent more hours per week on housework in 1960s (fifty-five) than they did in 1924 (fifty-two). Social expectations tend to ratchet up alongside technological proficiency. If it now takes half the time it used to take to hoover—well, you'll just be expected to hoover twice as much. Hester and Srnicek give a deadpan account of a 1940s advertisement for a washing machine: "once the clothes are in the washing machine," says the delighted customer, "I'm free [sic] . . . to do other housework." Automated reproductive labor, then, doesn't guarantee more free time; we must also lower our collective standards. (That's good news for slobs like me: crumpled clothes, hairy legs, and messy houses can be figured as a kind of a kind of lo-fi political resistance.)

Nonetheless, Hester and Srnicek do still have a somewhat coarse view of the relationship between technology and freedom. For Hester and Srnicek, technology expands the realm of freedom. It does this by adding new options. Without a dishwasher, I have no choice but to do the dishes. But once I have a dishwasher—here they quote Martin Hägglund—"doing dishes by hand is not a necessity but a choice."

The example is not as compelling as it might seem. I once could have traveled by horse and carriage from Oxford to London, but thanks to the internal combustion engine, the public infrastructure required for such a trip to be feasible no longer exists. The United

States' car-focused public infrastructure prevents its citizens from doing simple things, like walking to work. When it comes to social arrangements, technology both adds options and takes them away. It destroys some forms of compulsion while creating its own mandates. It need not roll back the sphere of necessity.

Hester and Srnicek might more be sanguine than most about automating *some* reproductive labor. But they are not sanguine about automating *all* of it. This technological remainder motivates a third move: *efficiency*. The basic social infrastructure of the Global North funnels reproductive labor into the sealed-off space of the household, which is tied to biogenetic kinship and "nuclear" living arrangements. This enclosure prevents specialization and (temporal) economies of scale: when everyone has their own kitchen, everyone has their own kitchen to clean. But such an arrangement is not inevitable; the atomic household needn't function as the default locus for care work. We might instead rely, as the United Kingdom did during World War II, on public canteens—decorated with art from Buckingham Palace—that cooked nutritious meals prepared at scale. (These "British Restaurants," Hester and Srnicek point out, were initially called "communal feeding centres," but the name was vetoed by Winston Churchill for "sounding too communist.")

It's helpful to situate this suggestion in terms of three social dynamics posited by Nancy Fraser. First, there is the struggle for social protection: demands for material security. Second, there is marketization: the tendency for more aspects of social life to be commodified. Third, there is the struggle for emancipation: demands that social hierarchies like those of race and gender be dismantled.

Fraser

Fraser notes that each of these forces is politically ambivalent. The family and the welfare state are iron fists as well as velvet gloves: they can offer protection, but they also discipline those who break its rules. Marketization breeds vulnerability, but it can also offer a route to freedom. You might, like me, prefer for your material security to depend on your earning power than on your ability to keep your husband happy. And emancipation struggles may weaken social bonds—and thus a basis of social protection—in the course of dismantling hierarchy.

In terms of this typology, *After Work* attempts to show that demands for social protection—specifically in the form of care—can be met without compromising on emancipation. Existing models of care provision tend heavily towards privatization: your care is either a business (traded on the open market), or nobody's business but yours (a family affair). *After Work* suggests a third option: care should be communal. Households should be more porous—for example, they should share communal goods and spaces—and they should no longer be the centers of gravity around which informal relations of care revolve. As a result, the burden of care is lifted from the household, but not offloaded onto the market. What's not to like?

Yet real life is messier than this solution allows. Communal spaces can be lovely; they can also be deeply unpleasant. I don't like cleaning my kitchen, but I also like not having to share it. When I read *After Work*, I was visiting my brother in Edinburgh, and we sat talking about it on the bus. He was enthusiastic about the idea that more of our lives should take place in shared spaces. Then a baby started to scream, and we couldn't talk for the rest of the journey. "I guess this is why people like cars," my brother said, darkly.

It could well be that other people's screaming children are a price worth paying for a functional care infrastructure. But there's no getting around the fact that there are costs to making our lives more communal. No transition to a post-work world is (democratically) possible unless people can be persuaded that the form of life on offer in the communal feeding center is a form of life that they would want.

Such persuasion might well be possible, but it's not a task that Hester and Srnicek really attempt. They do acknowledge that "not everybody would feel comfortable living in fully collectivized living spaces for any great length of time, and many will want more than a single bedroom to retreat to." And collective living, they are clear, "cannot be imposed from the top down." Hester and Srnicek argue that, if we want free time, we will need to live more communally. But what *they* take as an argument for more collective living, someone *else* might read as an argument against shrinking reproductive labor to a minimum. *After Work* maps the territory for political battle but doesn't begin to fight it.

THE BOOK'S VISION doesn't end here. Hester and Srnicek realize that while we might be able to shrink the amount of reproductive labor that needs to get done, we can't shrink it to zero. So alongside their main approach—lessening the burden—they offer two other strategies.

Fraser

The first is to incorporate care work into their picture of flourishing: what it means to live a good life. In a truly just society, this strategy says, caring labor will no longer be alienating, because we will value service to others—either for its own sake, or as part of an authentically valued project. In the lesbian separatist communities of second wave feminism—the landdyke commune, the Oregon-based "WomanShare"—participants dug ditches, converted livestock outbuildings into homes, and went in for low-tech farming. Under different conditions, such work could easily be alienating. But when folded into a larger political project to which the women freely subscribed, even their drudgery became meaningful—an *expression* of agency, rather than a straitening of it.

Wilde thought a post-work utopia would mean a world in which we are relieved of the "sordid" requirement to care for others and would be free to "realize" our own personalities. But Wilde got things back to front, say Hester and Srnicek. Caring for others is not a squalid compromise with scarcity; rather, we can realize our personalities by caring for others.

The analytic Marxist G. A. Cohen illustrated the logic of such arguments by analogy. Say we want a world where there's a plentiful supply of blood for transfusions, but also where no one is coerced into giving blood. It might seem that there is a tension between these two goals. But there isn't, Cohen says: if we create a culture in which people *want* to give blood, then we can have both blood and freedom. Similarly, *After Work* suggests, a just society will shape the souls of its citizens, so that they want to serve. One might wonder whether soul-making is really an alternative to coercion, rather than a particularly subtle form of it. But in Hester and Srnicek's hands, at least, it is not sinister social programing so much as the insight that necessary labor could be structured on "more agential terms," thus making it a more attractive pastime.

Besides, Hester and Srnicek are clear-eyed about the limits of any such transformation. They don't think that cleaning the toilet can be turned into a treat; they allow that some necessary labor will remain burdensome even in a post-work utopia. Its existence is compatible with freedom, they say, so long as we ought to divide that labor "equitably." Their picture, then, is one on which some reproductive labor may cease to be alienating because our attitudes toward it will be transformed. But there will still be some care work that no one chooses for its own sake. This brings us to their last strategy: the remaining work, they say, should be distributed equitably, divided "from each according to their abilities, to each according to their needs."

That's a nice enough slogan, but in *After Work* it never becomes a serious proposal. Suppose you work faster than I do. Do you have to work the same number of hours that I work, and therefore perform more tasks? Or do you have to complete the same number of tasks as I do, in which case I will have to work more hours?

Beyond this lack of detail, there is a more serious problem. Even in a perfectly just society, there will be people who just don't want to do any care work at all: they will prefer to freeride rather than do their fair share, whatever that turns out to be. Once we attend to would-be freeriders, it is not clear that a post-work society could really be a society of freedom, at least as Hester and Srnicek themselves understand it. As they put it, freedom entails that "the means of one's existence will never be at stake in any of one's relationships." But a society that relies on everyone doing their fair share of care work presumably couldn't get by without the resources to penalize those who opt out. And if a society has the means to impose such penalties, it will be a society in which the means of one's existence *can* be a stake in one's relationships. If we really want an equitable division of care work, some people will need to be coerced into doing it.

Hester and Srnicek might concede that *perfect* freedom is not compatible with care for all, but at least we would be much freer in a post-work society than we are now. (Perhaps more political theorists should be Winnicottians—concerned with developing the "good-enough" society.) So long as we have sufficient time to choose and pursue our own projects, it should not matter too much that there will still be allotments of necessity: parcels of time that are not truly our own. And, perhaps, these refractory parcels could even be packaged as a feature, rather than a bug.

For Hester and Srnicek, freedom and necessity are like land and sea—one a hospitable dwelling-place, the other a hostile territory. They think that with some ingenuity we can wall ourselves off from the water. For my part, I see human life as lived in a sort of tidal zone—an in-between place, with its own alluvial treasures. Necessity can serve as a spur to moral learning, wresting us from or filling out a cramped set of values. We often discover the projects that give shape and meaning to our lives only because we stumble into them, forced into roundabout routes by a fractal floodplain. We want to author our own lives, yes. But the value of some activities is opaque until we try them: it can't be grasped in advance.

The actor Sally Phillips, who has a son with Down's syndrome, puts the point perfectly. "I have such a rich life," she says. "They say the special needs club is one that nobody wants to join, but once you do, you realize you're in it with the best people in the world." If an expansion of the realm of freedom is an expansion of the realm of choice, then perfect freedom might, in effect, exile us from certain forms of goodness. A life composed only of self-realization will tend to create a self of the sort that doesn't deserve to be realized. Unwanted work can serve as a teacher, shushing the would-be brat that lurks in every human heart. Communal life presupposes a deep structure of *Bildung*, through which we become fitted as companions for others.

WHEN WE REFLECT on the two-facedness of necessity—on the ways it serves us, as well as on the ways it does us damage—we come up against the limits of *After Work*'s politics. Hester and Srnicek's preferred rubrics—*free time, self-realization*—can't distinguish between just and unjust forms of compulsion.

When a sulky teenager is made to set the table by her parents, her labor is alienated; she would rather be doing something else. Her activity is unchosen and imposed; she refuses to avow the purposes it serves. But to know whether the teenager is wronged, it is not enough to know how she *feels* about setting the table. Rather, we need to ask questions like: Does the teenager's work benefit a community that is oriented toward her flourishing? Does the community weigh her claims and interests equally to those of its other members? Does she

Fraser

have a meaningful say over its policies, priorities, and direction? Or does it serve a community who dominates her, who sweeps her along while blocking their ears to her claims and interests?

The answers make a difference to the character of the compulsion (as more sophisticated theorists of alienation acknowledge). Someone whose work serves a democratic community—a community for which they serve as a trustee, rather than merely as a mute resource—is not wronged, regardless of whether her work is dull or stimulating, cherished or resented. Conversely, feeling happy about one's work is no antidote to victimization. Someone who cares for her baby because she loves him can still be an exploited worker. Her love, although it benefits the baby, *also* benefits Jeff Bezos and Mark Zuckerberg, by creating a future worker and consumer, from whom they can harvest data, and profit. (This is the trick of capitalism: it takes our freedom and turns it against our deepest interests.)

Because Hester and Srnicek take choice as the measure of emancipation, they end up saying relatively little about the broader social relations in which labor should be embedded. Yet social relations are the real springs and cogs of justice. What really matters, when it comes to work, is not whether we can realize ourselves through it or whether we identify with its purposes. It's the social relations that wrench us into motion. Without a way to talk about these forces, we will go on misdiagnosing the real pathologies of our contemporary work regime.

THE STATE AGAINST ABOLITION
Azadeh Shahshahani

ON JANUARY 18 Atlanta police, DeKalb County police, Georgia state troopers, and a SWAT team descended on a protest encampment armed with dogs, pepper bullets, and live ammunition. They shot and killed twenty-six-year-old Manuel Paez Terán (also known as Tortuguita), a young Indigenous Venezuelan who had been protesting the clearing of forest to build the Atlanta Public Safety Training Center, known to those who have spent the past two years opposing it as Cop City.

Even after their death—which Kamau Franklin of the group Community Movement Builders, a Black, member-based collective of community residents and organizers, rightly called a "political assassination"—the officers continued with the violent clearing operation, cutting tree limbs and ropes from under tree sitters and attacking protesters with rubber bullets and tear gas. The official autopsy, finally released in April, reveals that Tortuguita was shot over fifty times. Researchers and journalists have called the shooting "unprecedented." According to *The Guardian*, it is the first known instance of state forces in the United States killing an environmental protester.

Just eleven days after Tortuguita's murder, two water defenders from Guapinol, Honduras, Aly Domínguez and Jairo Bonilla, were assassinated by unidentified gunmen. The two cofounded a group responsible for leading an occupation of the Los Pinares mine to protest against exploitative mining operations which would pollute their water source, the Guapinol River. The Honduran government has refused to investigate the matter further, instead blaming the murders on a robbery attempt.

Between December 2022 and February 2023, at least seven land defenders and community members across the Bajo Aguán region—a fertile and heavily militarized region in Northern Honduras—were killed, including campesino leader Hipolito Rivas of the Gregorio Chavez Cooperative, his son Jose Omar Cruz Tome, president of the Los Laureles cooperative, and his father-in-law, Andy Martinez Murrillo. For decades, communities in the Bajo Aguán and international solidarity organizations have denounced the collaboration between private security firms working for palm oil and mining corporations and military and police-backed paramilitary forces heavily supported by the United States to violently repress organized opposition to the land theft and environmental destruction upon which the industries depend.

Meanwhile, in northern El Salvador, just a week before the deadly raid in the Weelaunee forest, state police were engaged in a raid of their own. Residents of the rural community of Santa

Marta awoke in the middle of the night to sirens and floodlights as police arrested Antonio Pacheco, the executive director of the Association of Economic and Social Development (ADES) of Santa Marta, who helped lead El Salvador's powerful anti-mining movement. Four other community leaders—Miguel Ángel Gámez, Alejandro Laínez García, Pedro Antonio Rivas Laínez, and Saúl Agustín Rivas Ortega—were also arrested. The scene was all too familiar to a community that suffered a horrific massacre and brutal state violence during El Salvador's U.S.-backed war against leftist revolutionary forces in the 1980s.

So while the Georgia State Patrol's murder of Tortuguita marks a grave first in the United States, the killing of land defenders is heartbreakingly common in South and Central America. Latin America has long been the deadliest region for human rights and environmental defenders. In its 2022 analysis, Frontline Defenders noted that four out of the five countries contributing to 80 percent of the murders of human rights defenders worldwide that year were in Latin America. Other reports show that 75 percent of all killings of environmental activists worldwide have occurred there, and that it is particularly deadly for indigenous environmental activists. These statistics reveal what land defenders across the world have long known: state violence against environmental protesters is not confined to the United States.

But if not exclusively contained within its borders, the United States certainly has had an active role in its spread. It has a long history in Latin America of promoting economic policies to benefit corporations engaged in extractive and otherwise exploitative in-

Shahshahani

dustries, while simultaneously training, arming, and supporting the state and paramilitary forces that brutally repress those who resist such policies. In short, the U.S. brand of policing—the kind that would be taught and exported from Cop City—exists to protect capital and property. The crackdown against those fighting it, in Atlanta and in Honduras, El Salvador, and across the world, offers a frightening glimpse into a potential future: one of increasing state violence against communities everywhere who struggle to defend water, land, and ecosystems from corporate greed.

IN ATLANTA communities have been organizing to protect roughly ninety acres of the South River Forest, known to the Muscogee (Creek) people as Weelaunee Forest, not from the ravages of mining, palm oil plantations, logging, or hydroelectric dams—the major forces behind land grabs in Central America—but from the construction of a police base. The City of Atlanta, the Atlanta Police Department, and the Atlanta Police Foundation (APF) developed the idea for the Atlanta Public Safety Training Center after the 2020 uprisings against police violence. Its plans feature an explosives testing area, over twelve firing ranges, a Black Hawk helicopter landing pad, a training center to practice crowd control, a driving course for police to practice chases, and a "mock village" with a hotel, nightclub, and convenience store. Cop City, twice as large as facilities in New York and Los Angeles, would be the largest of its kind nationwide.

In September 2021 the Atlanta City Council approved the facility by a 10–4 vote and leased the land to the APF, a nonprofit organization that funnels private money to policing and surveillance of Atlanta residents. Supporters argue that current training facilities are "substandard," and that the center is necessary to boost police morale and retention. Residents opposed Cop City during seventeen hours of recorded public comment in 2021 and again in 2023.

The construction would deplete Atlanta's tree canopy and increase air and noise pollution for the majority Black and working-class neighborhood by the forest. Weapons testing and the shooting range will release heavy metals and toxic chemicals to the already endangered South River which will remain in the soil and water for decades. And Cop City's estimated $90 million price tag—$30 million from the City of Atlanta and $60 million from APF—does not account for the project's social and ecological costs.

Cop City is intended to intimidate and hinder movement building, divert much-needed resources away from communities, and exacerbate the surveillance of Black, brown, and other dispossessed communities—not only in Atlanta but across the country and around the world. Organizers recognize the threat that Cop City poses and have mobilized to oppose increased surveillance and police militarization as well as to protect the forest. But the state also recognizes the threat that these organizers pose to its efforts and has moved swiftly to leverage national and state counterterrorism measures against them, aiming to criminalize protest and discourage dissent.

Shahshahani

The state frequently deploys terrorism as a political label to justify violence against Black and Brown communities. Recently, local Georgia officials and prosecutors have described the prison abolitionist movement as a domestic terror threat, harkening back to 2020, when law enforcement units labeled Black Lives Matter and antifa protests as acts of domestic terrorism. During the "Green Scare" in the mid 2000s, the government prosecuted environmental activists with the Earth Liberation Front and Animal Liberation Front under federal terrorism laws, and ecoterrorism became the top domestic terrorism priority of the Department of Justice. In the late 2010s, the FBI began to classify and further surveil Black Lives Matter organizers as "Black identity extremists." More recently, organizers protesting the Dakota Access Pipeline have been prosecuted as terrorists.

Now, for the first time, Georgia is using its state domestic terrorism statute against an environmental or antiracist movement. Nearly twenty forest defenders were arrested under the statute between December 2022 and January 2023, a number that has since risen to over forty. Police affidavits cite "criminally trespassing on posted land," "sleeping in the forest," "sleeping in a hammock with another defendant," or being a "known member" of a "prison abolition movement" and "occupying a treehouse while wearing a gas mask and camouflage clothing" as examples of "terrorist" activity. Even bail fund organizers were arrested during a May 31 raid on the Atlanta Solidarity Fund office, facing charges of "charity fraud" and "money laundering."

Organizers and lawyers had previously warned that Governor Brian Kemp's "domestic terrorism" law would have disastrous implications for organizers and are now sounding the alarm over the dangerous legal precedent these charges may set. Under the Georgia statute, domestic terrorism now includes the commission of a felony with the intent to "disable or destroy critical infrastructure," causing "major economic loss," and (a) intimidate the civilian population, (b) alter, change, or coerce government policy, or affect the conduct of the government with the use of "destructive devices." "Critical infrastructure" could be public or private "facilities, systems, functions, or assets," physical or virtual, and provide or distribute "services for the benefit of the public." Already, twenty states have enacted similar anti-protest laws to quash environmental defenders.

Local officials in Georgia adopted language about "outside protesters" to justify a "state of emergency" in response to the ongoing resistance to Cop City and the protests after Tortuguita was killed. On January 26 Kemp issued an executive order granting him expansive powers, including the deployment of up to one thousand National Guard troops to "subdue riot and unlawful assembly." And on August 29, state Attorney General Chris Carr charged sixty-one people, including organizers, a legal observer, and bail fund workers, under Georgia's Racketeer Influenced and Corruption (RICO) Act, issuing an indictment that links protests related to Stop Cop City with those that occurred in 2020 following the murder of George Floyd. Many of the named defendants are also facing simultaneous domestic terrorism charges, setting a dangerous precedent for the use of RICO to stifle dissent.

THIS NEW REALITY for U.S. environmental activists is one that organized popular movements in Central America, where the police and military have received extensive U.S. training for decades, know all too well.

As in Atlanta, accusations of terrorism have been used to dehumanize the state's enemies. In El Salvador's case, environmental activists and community leaders have been labeled as gang members. The charges have also been deployed to justify and glamorize state violence, with government photographs of masses of handcuffed prisoners circulated to simultaneously invoke fear and normalize degradation. The government calls its new prison, claimed to be one of the largest in the world, the "Terrorist Confinement Center." Against this backdrop, the Bukele regime has arrested not only anti-mining activists, but also union leaders, youth organizers, and political opponents.

The attorney general's operation against the Santa Marta Five, as the jailed anti-mining protesters have come to be known, occurred amid a campaign of massive arrests launched in March 2022, when the government of Nayib Bukele suspended key constitutional rights under the pretext of combating gang violence. Legislators from Bukele's party have continuously—and illegally—reapproved a thirty-day emergency measure known as a state of exception for the past sixteen months. The Salvadoran government's steamrolling of due process has become a nightmare for working-class families whose communities have been militarized, with over 71,000 people arrested, many without warrants, evidence, or investigation. By July 2023 Salvadoran human rights organizations had documented over

6,400 human rights violations, mainly arbitrary arrests, and the deaths of at least 153 people in prison, whether from torture, beatings, or lack of access to medical care. None had been found guilty of a crime.

These policies are the culmination of two decades of U.S.-backed repressive policing. As scholars Leisy Abrego and Steven Osuna outline, right-wing governments first implemented an "iron fist" antigang plan in El Salvador "modeled on U.S. zero-tolerance policies and broken windows policing" in 2003. Like the counter-insurgency campaigns of the 1980s, the U.S. policing and security strategies exported over the past thirty years have armed governments throughout Central and South America with tools to repress impoverished communities, including those organizing to defend land and water.

In 2006 the far-right Nationalist Republican Alliance administration passed an antiterrorism law modeled closely on the USA Patriot Act. Grassroots organizers in El Salvador loudly opposed the law for its sweeping nature, warning it would open the door to political persecution. Among the first people to be charged under the new statutes were fourteen community activists from the community of Suchitoto who were protesting water privatization. Accompanied by successful international solidarity efforts, they were freed in 2007 and charges were dropped.

The training of security forces in South and Central America is a pillar of U.S. geopolitical strategy in the region: it ensures that those in power remain friendly to U.S. business interests. The infamous School of the Americas, first based in Panama and later relocated to Fort Moore, Georgia (and subsequently rebranded to the "Western Hemisphere institute for Security Cooperation" after being accused of training its graduates in torture and assassination techniques), hosts South and Central American military officers and offers courses from "tactical training to advanced theory on the application of military doctrine." Among the school's graduates in El Salvador are Col. Domingo Monterrosa, who led the infamous Atlácatl Battalion that massacred hundreds in El Mozote in 1981, and Roberto D'Aubuisson, who planned the 1980 assassination of Salvadoran archbishop Óscar Romero, an outspoken critic of the military government. The institute remains operational and reports "graduating 1,200–1,900 military, police, and civilian students from across the Hemisphere annually."

In the mid-2000s, the United States expanded its focus more specifically to policing. In 2005, as part of an effort to shore up confidence for U.S. investors in the newly-passed Dominican Republic-Central America Free Trade Agreement, the Bush administration opened a new branch of the Clinton-era international police training school, the International Law Enforcement Academy (ILEA), in San Salvador. The United States frames this work as police "professionalization"—a suspect term, considering the fact that the United States remains the high-income country with by far the highest rate of police killings in the world. What's been called the "School of the Americas for police" has graduated thousands of police officers throughout Central and South America who receive training from the FBI, DEA, and other agencies based in the United States, including state and local police forces. As of 2011, these trainings also include courses led by the Atlanta Police Department, through its partnership with the State Department.

In 2007 the Bush administration launched the Mérida Initiative, said to focus on border surveillance and assisting Mexican and other Central American governments in the War on Drugs. Experts argued early on that it would merely strengthen organized crime networks and were soon proven right. The Central America Regional Security Initiative soon followed, purporting to "stop the flow of narcotics, arms, weapons, and bulk cash generated by illicit drug sales" and "[strengthen] and [integrate] security efforts from the U.S. Southwest border to Panama."

By 2017 the Inter-American Commission on Human Rights was hearing cases regarding rising numbers of extrajudicial killings at the hands of Salvadoran police, and by 2018 the United Nations Special Rapporteur on extrajudicial, summary and arbitrary executions reported "a pattern of behavior amongst security personnel, amounting to extrajudicial executions and excessive use of force," citing "elements of the legal framework, such as the 2006 Counter-terrorism Law," as key contributors to these violations.

A key component of U.S. police reform efforts in Central America has been to create, develop and train elite police units to specialize in the fight against organized crime—often to deadly ends. Investigators connected El Salvador's Specialized Reaction Forces, a joint police and military unit backed by significant U.S. funding, to the murder of forty-three suspected gang members in the first half of 2017 alone. Though officially disbanded, many of its members transitioned to a new U.S.-backed unit, the Jaguars. In neighboring Honduras, the United States heavily invested in the creation of the

TIGRES (Intelligence Troops and Specialized Security Response Groups). Launched in 2012, TIGRES officers have, on multiple occasions, been implicated in drug trafficking, corruption, and state repression of protesters.

In recent years, some of the most notorious U.S.-trained security forces around the world have become the trainers, often with funding from various U.S. agencies. Colombian soldiers now offer trainings in Honduras through the United States Southern Command (SOUTHCOM). The Atlanta police, too, have received training from Colombia, as well as from Israel and elsewhere, through a program subsidized by the U.S. Department of Justice. Activists have argued that, if built, Cop City might host similar trainings for international forces.

Through U.S.-funded training and capacity-building programs, many of the most dangerous elements of policing practices now circulate internationally. Since the founding of U.S.-backed police schools in El Salvador, the country's incarceration rate per capita surpassed that of the United States; it is now the highest in the world.

When Salvadoran president Nayib Bukele appeared on Tucker Carlson's show on Fox News to celebrate his crackdown, he exhorted the United States to follow in his footsteps. Amid ongoing protests against Cop City, Kemp welcomed Salvadoran ambassador Milena Mayorga to Georgia in March. That same month Mayorga would go on to invite Atlanta mayor Andre Dickens to visit El Salvador on an upcoming delegation. As Georgia and the Salvadoran government forge stronger diplomatic ties, the U.S. export of "expertise" to police and military in Central America is no longer a straight line but has instead come full circle.

FIFTEEN YEARS AGO the directors of ILEA were remarkably clear when discussing their goals for opening a new police training academy in El Salvador: to make Latin America "safe for foreign investment" by "providing regional security and economic stability and combating crime." Such comments were recently echoed by Laura Richardson, head of SOUTHCOM for Latin America, when she framed the importance of U.S. military operations in Latin America in terms of the region's "rich resources and rare earth elements," like lithium and oil.

It's not a coincidence that corporations from Wells Fargo to Axon, the manufacturers of tasers, have been major donors to the Atlanta Police Foundation for the construction of Cop City and to police foundations across the country. Like the police they fund, they know that the battles over access to land and natural resources will only increase as the climate crisis intensifies, and they are acting accordingly.

But there is some room for hope. The Defend the Atlanta Forest/ Stop Cop City movement, guided by antiracist, Indigenous, abolitionist principles and environmental politics, has successfully halted the project thus far, with the help of protesters who have occupied the forest since late 2021. These defenders use a variety of tactics: encampments, tree-sits, peaceful marches, community events, and investigative research. The initial and ongoing resistance has forced the city to reduce the project's scale from over 150 acres to 85 and promise to preserve the surrounding forest as a 265-acre public park.

Land and water defenders in El Salvador, too, have successfully prevented mining operations. In 2017, the country became the first in the world to ban metal mining, due in large part to the communities who worked relentlessly for nearly two decades to organize against it, despite threats and harassment. Other communities and movements throughout the region are following suit, refusing to give in to coercive and violent U.S.-backed military and paramilitary forces. In a 2015 case in Honduras, the Inter-American Commission on Human Rights found that the state violated the human rights of the indigenous Garifuna communities by expanding urban developments into the community's land. This decision marked a victory for the recognition of Garifuna land rights, though the Honduran government has yet to implement any measures in accordance with the decision.

Environmental movements have also been able to fight back against the criminalization of land and water defenders. After an international outcry, the charges against eight water defenders from Guapinol, arrested in 2019 for opposing the Los Pinares mining project, were dropped in 2022. And on September 5 the five Santa Marta water defenders arrested in January were moved from prison to house arrest following an international campaign, though the struggle to drop all the charges against them continues.

The United States' investment in controlling territories, resources, and entire populations through policing now mirrors the tactics that it helped usher into existence in Central America. This indicates that movements in both the United States and Central America have posed significant challenges to the prevailing racialized order. Despite the risks, organized communities in Central America are not backing down. Nor are the organizers in Atlanta. Together they are envisioning urgently needed alternatives to both environmental destruction and militarization.

The author would like to thank the Committee in Solidarity with the People of El Salvador for their contributions toward research for this article.

Shahshahani

CONTRIBUTORS

Elisabeth R. Anker is Professor of American Studies and Political Science at George Washington University. Her latest book is *Ugly Freedoms*.

Lorna N. Bracewell is Associate Professor of Political Science at Flagler College and author of *Why We Lost the Sex Wars: Sexual Freedom in the #MeToo Era*.

Jefferson Cowie received the 2023 Pulitzer Prize in History for *Freedom's Dominion: A Saga of White Resistance to Federal Power*. He teaches at Vanderbilt University.

Nathalie Etoke is Associate Professor of Francophone and Africana Studies at the Graduate Center of the City University of New York. Her latest book is *Black Existential Freedom*.

Rachel Fraser is Associate Professor of Philosophy at the University of Oxford.

Adom Getachew is Neubauer Family Assistant Professor of Political Science at the University of Chicago and author of *Worldmaking after Empire: The Rise and Fall of Self-Determination*.

Lewis Gordon is Board of Trustees Distinguished Professor of Philosophy and Global Affairs at the University of Connecticut. His latest book is *Fear of Black Consciousness*.

Nancy J. Hirschmann is Geraldine R. Segal Professor in American Social Thought at the University of Pennsylvania. Her latest book is *Gender, Class, and Freedom in Modern Political Theory*.

Will Holub-Moorman is a PhD student in history at Princeton and a Digital Fellow at the Society for the History of Children and Youth.

Travis Knoll teaches history at Wingate University. His writing has also appeared in *Jacobin* and the *Washington Post*.

Hannah Liberman is a writer and editor. She is an MFA candidate in the Programs in Writing at UC Irvine.

Tamara Metz is Associate Professor of Political Science and Humanities at Reed College and author of *Untying the Knot: Marriage, the State and the Case for Their Divorce*.

A. Dirk Moses is Anne & Bernard Spitzer Chair in International Relations at the City College of New York, editor of the *Journal of Genocide Research*, and author of *The Problems of Genocide: Permanent Security and the Language of Transgression*.

Samuel Moyn is Chancellor Kent Professor of Law and History at Yale University. His latest book is *Liberalism Against Itself: Cold War Intellectuals and the Making of Our Times*.

Philippe Van Parijs is Professor of Economic, Social, and Political Sciences at the University of Louvain and a research fellow at Nuffield College, Oxford. His books include *Real Freedom for All*.

Mark Paul is Assistant Professor at the Edward J. Bloustein School of Planning and Public Policy at Rutgers and author of *The Ends of Freedom: Reclaiming America's Lost Promise of Economic Rights*.

Aziz Rana, incoming J. Donald Monan, S.J., University Professor of Law and Government at Boston College Law School, is author of *The Two Faces of American Freedom*. His book *The Constitutional Bind: How Americans Came to Idolize a Document That Fails Them* will be released in 2024.

William Clare Roberts is Associate Professor of Political Science at McGill. He is working on a book called *The Radical Politics of Freedom*.

Julie Rose is Associate Professor of Government at Dartmouth and author of *Free Time*.

Azadeh Shahshahani is Legal & Advocacy Director at Project South and a past president of the National Lawyers Guild.

Olúfẹ́mi O. Táíwò is Associate Professor of Philosophy at Georgetown. His latest book is *Reconsidering Reparations*.

Lea Ypi is Professor of Political Theory at the London School of Economics. Her latest book is *Free: Coming of Age at the End of History*.

About the Cover Art
The quilt featured on the cover, *"Bars" Work-Clothes Quilt*, was made by Loretta Pettway in Boykin, Alabama. She is a member of the Gee's Bend Collective, a community of Black artists whose quilting practices stretch back to the nineteenth century. Her work has been shown at the Whitney Museum and the Metropolitan Museum of Art.